THOUGHT LEADER ACADEMY

10X YOUR IMPACT AND INCOME THROUGH YOUR MISSION AND MESSAGE

SARA CONNELL

Thought Leader Academy: 10x Your Impact and Income
Through Your Mission and Message

Copyright © 2023 by Sara Connell

All rights reserved. No part of this publication may be reproduced, distributed, or transmitted in any form or by any means, including photocopying, recording or other electronic or mechanical methods, without the prior written permission of the author, except in the case of brief quotations embodied in reviews and certain other non-commercial uses permitted by copyright law.

Printed in the United States of America

Hardback ISBN: 978-1-960876-36-2
Hardcover ISBN: 978-1-960876-37-9
Paperback ISBN: 978-1-960876-38-6
Ebook ISBN: 978-1-960876-39-3

Library of Congress Control Number: 2023945501

Muse Literary
3319 N. Cicero Avenue
Chicago IL 60641-9998

The information in this book is intended for educational and entertainment purposes only. This book is not intended to be a substitute for legal, medical, psychological, accounting, or financial advice of a professional. The author and publisher are not offering professional service advice. Additionally, this book is not intended to serve as the basis for financial and business decisions. You should seek the services of a competent professional in making all decisions specific to your situation.

Success and results shared are not typical and do not guarantee future results or performance. Some names and distinguishing characteristics of people represented in this book have been changed to respect confidentiality. The Thought Leaders Academy member stories shared in the final section of this book feature the real names and specifics of each leader and are told by the members, in their own words.

While best efforts have been made while preparing this book, the author and publisher make no warranty, representation, or guarantee with respect to the accuracy or completeness of information contained herein.

The author and publisher assume no responsibility for your actions and specifically disclaim responsibility for any liability, loss, risk, or physical damages, personal or otherwise, which is incurred as a consequence directly or indirectly of the use and application of the content of this book.

> *"Do you have the courage to bring forth this work? The treasures that are hidden inside you are hoping you will say yes."*
> —**Elizabeth Gilbert,** *Big Magic*

Dedication

To YOU! For the books, talks, and genius you will create. It matters. You matter. Thanks to your contribution, the world will never be the same.

To ensure you get maximum positive impact and results from reading this book, I've created a portal of goodies, bonus materials, and resources.

Access the workbook, guided trainings, interviews, and bonuses for this book FREE at our Thought Leader book portal here:

Introduction

During the last week of fourth grade, I saw a flyer posted on a bulletin board at our local library. The paper was kelly green and embossed on the top was an illustration of a man with a three corner hat blowing into a bugle. The flyer announced open auditions for *The Pied Piper* at The Children's Theater of Arlington. Looking at that jaunty page, I was struck by the sensation I would later come to call *Resonance*. The library walls seemed to expand and contract, the ding of the silver attention bell, the whine of hungry toddlers, mothers shushing- all faded into a whispering hum, as my vision fixated on that piece of green paper.

I hadn't heard of The Children's Theater, but my chest began to warm and my nerves tingled from my heart to my fingers. My body knew, before my mind could even catch up, that I needed to know this place, to be in that play. I had the feeling that somehow the Children's Theater of Arlington was a magic that I must taste, that it held some piece of my destiny.

The librarian pulled the flyer off the board to show me the date for the auditions had passed. "They do several shows a year," she said. "You can try out for the next one in the fall."

All summer I begged my mother to take me to the library to check the board (no Internet yet). Finally one day, like a mirage in the one hundred degree humidity of late August in Northern Virginia, a fuchsia paper blazed on the spongy cork. This time the play was *Peach Boy*, a fable from northern China. I made it to the final round of auditions but not into the cast and was gutted. The desire to be inside the hidden theater world had only grown stronger. I'd played the lead in every school production since kindergarten. I didn't know what I'd done wrong. December peeled into January and a new play was announced. *Sleeping Beauty* flyers went up on turquoise paper. The silhouette image of a girl in front of a sewing wheel and tiny fairies flying around her head beckoned to me. For months, pacing back and forth in my bedroom, I'd worked on diction, projection, singing (many of the plays were musicals), and dance. My mother showed me the story of Euripides who stuffed his mouthful of rocks so he could become a master orator. I didn't use rocks, but I liked his obsession.

I made it through the first round, then callbacks. Finally the director, a chic woman with a grey bob and silk scarf tied around her shoulders, walked a group of ten kids down a long hallway of the middle school where the auditions were held. The walls were heavy beige cement, the old tile floor worn and scuffed with countless shoes. "I'm going all the way to the other end," she said. "We'll be performing in a big theater," she said. "Hundreds of seats. When I call your name, say anything you want, so I can test your ability to project your voice. People will need to hear you in the back rows."

What I remember is feeling as if the happiness for the rest of my life hung on what would come out of my mouth.

What my mother remembers is sitting in the waiting room with two dozen other parents when the soft hum of a radiator was interrupted by my voice roaring down the hall, "MY NAME IS SARA AND I REALLY WANT TO BE IN THIS PLAY!"

I was cast as a fairy and I went on to perform in those Children's Theater plays and then in Shakespeare in the Park and even teen politics show on CNBC, in courtroom dramas and high school musicals and every production I could get my hands on for the next ten years.

Have you had a Resonance moment? Felt the tingling, demanding, that won't let you go no matter how hard you try to push it away, this is my destiny? Was there something you came across that grabbed you by the spine and said, "You will follow me, you must follow me. For this you have come!"

Maybe you feel that right now. You picked up this book because you know there's a bigger stage (literal or metaphoric) you NEED to be on, a greater impact you must fulfill, more of your potential and gifts and talents and genius that (despite what those mean critic voices in your head like to say), you KNOW the world needs at this time.

Maybe your early resonance moments, those that imprinted you with

INTRODUCTION

your life purpose, rose out of joy like the theater flyer in the library or through adversity like my friend who remembers her mother shaking her awake in the middle of the night and sleeping in the car to escape her father's fists. Maybe you experienced the seeds of your calling like one of my clients who moved from Eastern Europe to America at the age of ten and went on to become a scientist, then an executive at a tech company where she always felt like the "other" and where she was the only woman in the room.

My lense in life at the moment of finding the Children's Theater was that of a white, middle class, girl. I had the privilege of my ethnicity, parents that would drive me to rehearsals, an abundance of food, a safe place to sleep at night and far more. I wrote about the Children's Theater for a school paper in eighth grade and the teacher wrote "give me something real" in his note at the end. I wasn't ready to write about the rape I'd experienced at 8, the assaults I would reckon with finally in my twenties and thirties. I wouldn't dare share the addictions, the trauma legacy that also ran through our family's veins. Both the ecstasy of creative calling and the sledgehammer of trauma shaped my path. Being white, female, and American means I represent only a tiny fraction of experiences and worldviews. This is why the stories you'll read in this book and hear directly from our Thought Leader Academy members at the end represent a far wider spectrum of life, background and truth. I've coached women in their teens and women in their eighties. Women who fled home at sixteen and built businesses from nothing and women with PhDs who are changing systems, policies and institutions from the inside out. Women from six continents and dozens of countries.

While I represent only one person, the strategies you will learn here work for all. Success is your birthright and my intention and commitment in this book is that you will exponentially increase yours using what calls to you in these pages. You will not just hear my story, you will hear the chorus of voices that are stepping into thought leader power. Collectively, we will change the planet and the future of our families, communities and world.

Back to my teenage years . . .

As much as I loved theater, by college, my creative obsession had shifted towards writing, insistent and demanding, like a hanging plant stretching all its branches towards the sun. But being part of that theater world, experiencing what it is to shine one's light in service to one bigger light, to express, to create, to collaborate, to contribute changed me forever and moved me forward on my path.

Resonance moments point us to our True North. The Aboriginal peoples of New Zealand speak of an invisible life destiny path called our "Songline."

I never lost my love of creating epic and transformational experiences for people. When I released acting, I endeavored to create that magic in books, articles, talks, workshops, and classes and coaching the way I do to this day.

Moments of Resonance, of magic, of destiny are real. I believe that if we stay open to them, we encounter and source and receive signs when it's time for the next big leap, or even a soul-aligning micro-hop. I believe when the leader is ready, the teacher, resource, guide, answer, and flashing neon arrow appears.

The fact that we are together right now is not random. You picked up this book, at this moment, on purpose, for a purpose. If you've been feeling the call (for a week or a year or decades), that you are called to take our work to a bigger audience, if you know you have a first or next great book in you, if truly bringing forth what Elizabeth Gilbert in *Big Magic* says, "the treasures waiting inside you," consider this book your bright kelly green flyer on the library bulletin board.

You'll know if this is your nudge, your affirmation, your magic eight ball, "signs point to yes" if you FEEL inside your body and soul that there's a next level of impact for you. That it's time to be where you've always visioned you "should" be. You know if you're meant for more, ready for more: more financial abundance, more visibility, more contribution, more impact. You know if you're ready to leap from underearning to making hundreds of thousands or millions of dollars per year.

You know if this is the time for your "reality" and your vision board to

INTRODUCTION

coincide in a cosmic WIN-WIN-WIN. (For you, the people you are here to serve, and the world!) You know if it's time to see a few more zeros in your Instagram follower numbers, to be speaking on the stages where you've previously sat in the audience. Time to live and play FULL OUT, contributing the brilliant ideas and passion and unique world view and strategies that only you are capable of sharing. By doing this, giving to EVERYONE, you encounter a spark of permission and motivation to bring forth their greatest light.

Is it grandiose to propose you are here to do this and do it NOW?

Our world has conditioned us to play small, to play things safe, to be seduced by a false, insidious idea that we are less than capable, worthy, excellent, extraordinary, and here to manifest all the greatness inside us. If you want spiritual ballast, there's that haunting parable where a woman dies and finds out, "good news, there's no hell, no damnation." But then she is shown what her life COULD have been, if she'd lived, loved, contributed, and received fully of what she was capable of, of what life has to offer.

What comes up for you when you hear that story? Even if you find it preachy and overly moralistic, I'm curious about your answer. Are you currently living, contributing, creating everything you're made of? Are you making the fullest impact and creating the maximum abundance you desire to create? Desire is the seed. Desire is the SIGN. It is the affirmation and sneak preview of what you're capable of being.

In the pages of this book, I'm inviting you to take a Shero's journey-to uncover and amplify your unique greatness, your genius, your purpose, and to take that into the world in a bigger way than you ever have before. I'm inviting you to step into your power and contribution as a thought leader.

I'm going to give you every fast track, time collapsing, big win creating strategy, practice, and move I know so you can bring forth and fulfill the destiny you are here to create. Whether you want to write your first, or next, bestselling book, speak in your community, get paid $20,000 for keynote talks, stand in that red circle on the TEDx stage, create a community of millions or make six, seven, or eight figures of income per year, what I will instruct you through in this book can help you make it happen.

People have paid me cumulatively millions of dollars to share these strategies and mindsets, so why would I put them here in this book?

It's because of what happened after I graduated myself from the magical world of theater, but before I availed myself in the magical vortex of thought leadership. When I left monologues and audition songs behind and began writing, no one thought I was gifted. I didn't know the craft and I'd developed a belief that if I wasn't instantly great at something, I wasn't deserving or capable of doing it. I gave my power away to decide my destiny to teachers and mentors and family and peers and most dangerously to the gremlins, and the faceless "they" of the Internet, the trolls. I washed around in a dark sea of self-doubt and shame, and on some days, a kind of numbing soul despair because there was that green paper again, calling me to something, but everywhere I looked I thought I saw messages of my own inadequacy, unimportance, and worthlessness. I changed my courses from writing to literature, so much safer to consume other people's work than face the rigours and discomfort of writing my own.

I took a shadow creative job in advertising, a step even further away from my passion. In the chill of those steel stairways, I was victim to a panoply of abusive and traumatizing experiences. I stopped nourishing myself, started wasting even my cells and bones away-an outer expression of the emptiness and pain I felt every time a hand was laid on me, a comment landed on me, every time someone treated me like a discardable object, even when I said, "nooooo."

I spiraled further and further away from what I loved, what mattered most, from the tiny voice that still poked through like a sliver of grass through cement saying, "You're here to write, to create, to contribute something meaningful."

You've probably experienced something like this too, if not in a job, or a relationship, with your family or at school. Somewhere most of us got dinged or even pummeled and it took something from you. It took your confidence, your self-worth, your knowing of your own brilliance.

INTRODUCTION

But you are a Shero, resilient as a sword, and even with all of what you've been through for your age, your race, your sexual orientation, your desires, your resources, your education, your sensitivity, your ability or lack of ability (determined of course by others), your intelligence, or what others deemed a lack of any of these things.

Two hundred million people in America right now say they want to write a book, and while it may seem that everyone you know is working on a book, almost none of them will finish or publish that book. If they do, they'll slap it up on Amazon and resent that their best friend and their cat are the only ones who read it.

We think, if "I write or speak it, they will come." But impact and income rarely work with creating the content alone. There's another beat, another part of the equation that we must express, the part most of us resist, or even dread. We must SHARE the work, we must become wildly, awesomely, omnipresent VISIBLE to those we are here to serve and transform and lead.

What got me out of that mountain mine shaft, deep pit of sickness and pain was a single book. One book called *Holy Hunger* by a woman named Margaret Bullitt-Jonas who I'd never met and still have not met. A book by a noncelebrity, "regular" person who worked through enough of her crap to sit down and write her story with so much courage and honesty that because of reading it, I didn't die.

Despite what your inner critic and imposter syndrome gremlins say, YOU are someone's Margaret Bullitt-Jonas. You would never have picked out this book if you were not meant to impact people like this. You are already a thought leader. I'm writing this book for you now so you can make good on answering the question the sublime poet Mary Oliver asks, "What will you do with your one wild and precious life?"

After *Holy Hunger* saved my life, I vowed to spend the rest of my life paying forward the gift of that experience. I spent over a decade discovering, training, creating, and honing the strategies, mindset paradigms, practices, visualizations, templates, and tools I teach in Thought Leader Academy and now teach in this book so that my clients and now YOU will impact the people who need you and change our world. I've been on *Oprah, Good Morning America, Katie Couric,* and *The View.* I've been published in *The New York Times* and spoken at TEDx and been featured in *Forbes* and *Entrepreneur* and been nominated for a National Book Award, and the best part is that now I coach our clients to fulfill these same kinds of dreams. Even better, I help our clients do in one year what took me over $100,000 in trainings and ten years to achieve. Collectively, I've helped thousands of women transform their lives with their missions, messages, and movements. These women have generated many millions of dollars between them, and most of us started with no resources or confidence or belief that we could do any of it.

YOU are now part of that gift and of this community. It is your divinely timed moment to share the gifts you are here to share, in a massive way.

So that's what we're going to do. I'm going to pretend you are a member of our Thought Leader Academy and I get to coach you like I coach our clients. I'm going to show you everything I can fit into the pages of this book on how to practice the first step in being a Thought Leader (leading your own thoughts), how to set your idea on fire in a bestselling book, how to craft a powerful talk that has those who hear you want to work with you, and how to position yourself as an irresistible expert for podcasts, conferences, and online events. I'm going to show you how to find, inspire, and lead the people you are here to serve and then how to monetize your mission and create thousands or hundreds of thousands or millions of dollars doing your passion, bringing forth your ideas, sharing your message, and how to have the TIME OF YOUR LIFE while doing it! We're going to journey through the five strategies of the Thought Leader Academy pathway so you can rise to the leader you came to this planet to be.

INTRODUCTION

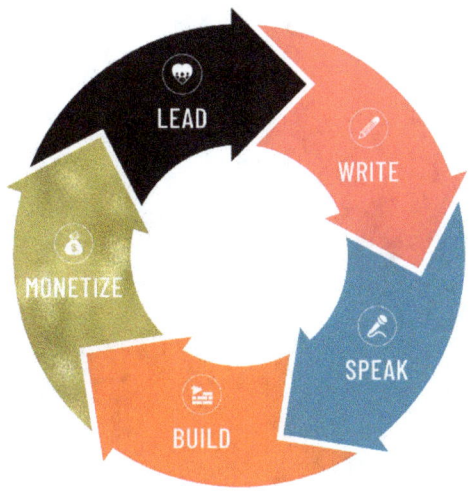

Have you felt your stomach twist when you see someone with a bigger following or see a colleague publish yet another bestselling book? Does your stomach sink when you log on to Zoom to teach a workshop or webinar and see just a few faces when inside you know you are here to serve thousands? Have you felt some stab of envy mixed with shame when you see other people launching programs and filling courses and posting, posting, posting their "success"? Has it hurt your heart when you stare across the gap between your life now and your vision board, sometimes so much that you tell yourself not to want the "next level" and to walk back, far back from your big goals? Have you told yourself that if "it" (the money, the impact, the publishing, and business success) hasn't happened yet, it likely won't, so what's the point in trying?

If you've experienced any of this, I'll tell you: there's nothing wrong with you. That pain is simply an indication of what you truly are and have not allowed yourself to be. A kind of Vision Anorexia that you get to break out of now. I get it. I spent almost twenty years denying my vision and then playing way too small. I've been down in that pit, and as another old story goes, the good thing about that is, I know the way out.

It's GO TIME and we don't have a minute to lose. The real you, your real life, is waiting. See you on the inside.

CHAPTER ONE

$20K to $2 Million

I never set out to start a company. The year I graduated from Northwestern University, I told people I wanted to move to London and be a writer. My grandmother bought me my first journal at five. I filled it with poems and drawings. I won the MS read-a-thon at my school every year. I devoured books the way my friends consumed Pixy Stix and M&M's. As a teenager, my idea of success was living in a garret apartment overlooking the Thames or the Seine, writing in the mornings, long walks along the river, eating soup out of the pot, books spilling over the couch cushions, late nights discussing art with friends, not much money, but deliriously happy, even before my big breakthrough to the *New York Times* bestseller list.

And I knew from reading books and watching movies that the way one knew she was destined to be a writer was that a teacher would take you aside and tell you, "you're special-you're meant to be an author!" After this benediction, you would ascend to the lofty ranks of Maya Angelou and Steven King.

The AP English teacher at my high school had published two books and had a column in *The Washington Post*. I believed his class would be my moment. But the famous teacher did not single me out. There was no "knighting," no secret handshake to induct me into the club. When this pivotal event failed to take place, I decided that I was not talented or good enough to be a writer, and so I went to college as an English major and spent four years reading other people's writing.

As college graduation approached, I knew what was expected of me. Most of the people in our extended family were doctors or lawyers. Many of the women stayed home with their kids. My father worked for the government in Washington DC. Jobs were real things, at companies or hospitals, with benefits and guaranteed paychecks. My confidence in my ability to "make it" as a writer was flimsy fantasy. After all, I already knew from the high school teacher, I wasn't worthy of being a published author. I'd never be successful as a writer.

So I took a job at a big advertising agency in Chicago. It was written up in magazines as "one of the top companies for women." The job offered a paycheck and benefits. It also offered rampant addiction, politics, and increasingly frequent sexual assaults.

I started binging on oversized bagels, deli sandwiches, pastries, anything I could scavenge from catering orders leftover from client meetings. I'd work until midnight, walk home, set my alarm for 5:00 a.m. so I could get up and run, to "burn it all off." Other days, I'd starve, waiting until 2:00 p.m. to eat and then only an apple only so I wouldn't faint in the afternoon meeting.

I cried so often in the stairwell that I wore the red paint off the railings and memorized the pattern in the tile floor. My friends and I began to call the agency The Dark Tower. Every day, when I walked through the onyx door, I felt like I was dying.

One day I ran through the Boston airport to catch my flight back to Chicago. In a blur, I saw a bookstore. I ran past the magazines, racks of chewing gum, Dramamine, and inflatable neck pillows to the new arrivals table. I didn't have time to read the back jackets or handwritten staff pics. I "randomly" grabbed the first book I saw, *Holy Hunger* by Margaret Bullitt-Jonas. I paid for the book and a roll of sugar-free lifesavers. I read the whole flight in the taxi ride home. I stayed up all night reading.

By the time I finished, shards of sunlight cut across my face. I didn't understand how or why, but I knew that I was done with that job. I was going to get help for the eating disorder. I found help, good help. I figured out ways to cobble together money for groceries. And what woke back up like a rising dragon was the desire to WRITE.

I still didn't feel worthy. I didn't think I would succeed. But by God, I was going to devote myself to paying the gift of that book forward. I vowed to bring out anything in me that could help another person the way Margaret Bullitt-Jonas had helped me.

I went through what we call in Thought Leader Academy: ALL IN.

It would be wonderful if we made an ALL IN declaration and success happened immediately. But three years into my "all in" writing commitment, I had almost nothing to show for my devotion. I had taken classes and developed a flow and worked up a manuscript and began, painfully, asking everyone I knew if they knew literary agents, a requirement for the path I'd identified for how to publish. Months later, someone I knew said he knew someone who knew an agent.

"She won't automatically take you on," he said. "But she'll probably take a phone call."

Before he hung up with me, he said, "It's good, right? Your writing? I don't want to blow my reputation with her."

My vocal chords strained. I wanted to say, "It's probably terrible. Don't introduce me."

But like the eleven-year-old girl in that middle school hallway trying out for the play, I heard myself say, "Yes."

The agent read my manuscript and said, "I have a bunch of revisions for you. If you're willing to make them, I'd be open to review and maybe, possibly, representing you."

A person with a burning vision to write books, who had wanted to write books since she was five, SHOULD have run home, put up a big 'Do Not Disturb' sign on the door and written feverishly through the night, by candlelight if necessary, hair wild around the face, like a Brontë heroine.

But I learned that week about the formidable power of resistance and fear. Instead of writing, I watched my laptop sit like a corpse in the center of my bedroom floor. A day went by, two days, two weeks. Three weeks. I could see I was going to lose this opportunity. I see the vision dissolving between my fingers.

I was confounded by my paralysis. I understand it perfectly now. If I tried, really gave it everything I had, and the agent rejected me, that would be it. The final nail in the coffin. The dream would be over.

I reminded myself that the dream would die anyway if I lost this opportunity, so I called a writing coach a friend had mentioned. I didn't want a coach. I didn't want to spend the money and the time and have someone see that I didn't know what I was doing. Thank God I called her anyway. Four months later, I flew to New York, and at a large wood table at the gorgeous Gramercy Tavern, the agent said the magic words I've held my breath to hear: Yes.

The manuscript got me a book deal, I went on *Oprah*, got published in *The New York Times*, and the day I received that *New York Times* check, a new vision emerged. The goal was no longer just about me and writing my books, I was now on a mission to amplify and empower other voices and callings-to get the methods, ideas, stories, and insight of the incredible leaders who are working with extraordinary skill, with soul, with heart, with purpose, into the hands of those who need them.

I knew this mission would require me to continually uplevel my psychology, spirit, and skill. I wanted the leaders I coached to receive world-class support. I studied storytelling, writing technique, and speaking with the top mentors I could find. I returned to Northwestern and got a masters in writing and teaching creative writing. I also understood viscerally that the work could not only be about craft and skill. I'd need to reverse engineer how we step into a new identity and unshackle ourselves from false ideas, societal conditioning, and past traumas because if ignored, these would stop me and any Thought Leader before they reached chapter two of their book. So, I studied neuroscience, mindset, psychology, quantum theory, spiritual practice. I trained with shamans, meditation experts, neuroscientists and became trained in NLP, hypnosis, and other brain-training modalities.

At the beginning, I focused exclusively on helping people write books. My very first client was a lawyer who hated her job. "I want to leave. I want to write full-time." The problem was, she didn't believe she could write a successful book. She felt trapped in her job. She wrote a few pages, then ignored her manuscript for months. She'd been trying to finish a book for four years. I related. I understood. By God, she was practically me five years earlier.

"This week, tell at least twenty people that you're a writer," I said.

She cringed.

"You'll block your success until you own it," I said. The research and brain study I'd done proved to me that identity drives behavior. I knew she could spend ten more years starting, stopping, unfilled like I'd been. I saw her talent. I felt the thrum of her vision.

"Fuck," she said. "I'll do it."

That week she told the grocery store checkout attendant, two women on the subway, a salesperson at Bath & Body Works and sixteen more people: "I am a writer." Two months later, she finished her book. I showed her how to pitch the book to publishers. Another month later, she had a book deal. By April, she was a number one bestseller on Amazon. She quit the law job, started her career as an author, and has never looked back.

WRITE

🙂 **You get great credibility as a bestselling author! You are the EXPERT on your topic and you are increasingly desirable as a speaker.**

☹️ Not enough people know about you or your book

A book is fantastic. It gives you instant credibility. You are seen as an expert because you literally "wrote the book" on your topic. But the problem is, if you want to be a thought leader and you have a BIG vision to serve large groups of people, the book alone may not get you the full impact you want.

I want to reach the maximum number of people who need what I share and teach. My clients do too. I reviewed my business to date and saw that I'd connected with nearly all of my clients through speaking to groups, presenting at events, and being interviewed on podcasts. I reverse engineered the process to help our clients do the same. We added speaking as the second thought leader strategy. When you add speaking, you are exponentially more visible. You're now an author-speaker. Double threat.

One of my clients was afraid of writing a book. She knew exactly what the book would be, she had an outline, even a chapter written. She had an incredible story of immigrating to America, overcoming prejudice, poverty, building a new life from scratch for her and her son. Then creating a successful business, helping parents support their children being who they are here to be, breaking ancestral trauma patterns, and creating healthy families. "English is my third language," she said. "The book won't be good. I'm better talking than I am writing." I was in awe of this woman. Writing in our first language was a challenge. I knew she would write a killer book. And, she needed to go in the order that called to her. So, we started with strategy two and went all in on booking her talks. She started with a few local talks and quickly she was speaking to larger audiences, then to an audience of one thousand. She was nominated for a TEDx talk. The day she stepped off that red circle with the glowing TEDx letters behind her, she called me. "I'm ready. I'm doing the book." Later that year, she had the bestselling book to go along with TEDx speaker. Double threat.

Speaking creates more credibility and visibility. You'll start attracting clients. AND, until you're speaking in NFL stadium Tony Robbins event-sized groups, you still won't have the fullest impact, still not reach everyone you're here to serve.

SPEAK

🙂 You're in front of more people (yea!) and you have exponential credibility as a bestselling author and demand speaker

☹ Only the people you're speaking to know about you so you're not getting the full impact and income you desire

So we added strategy three to the thought leader pathway: BUILD your audience. To take our clients to their next level of thought leadership, I immersed myself in mentorships and trainings on audience building. I discovered ways to find and build a community and audience without spending money on ads that I will teach you in this book. When you build a large audience, you add impact to the credibility and visibility you established through writing and speaking. It's amazing. Rocket fuel.

One of our clients had triumphed over stage 4 cancer. Before his book launched, we worked at building an audience. He had about one hundred people on an email list and almost no social media following. We focused on the strategies I'll teach you in the build section of this book. He hosted a summit, created joint ventures with aligned companies and leaders, and created valuable free content linked to a sign-up page. I showed him a strategy I'd use to inspire influencers to share his message and book with their large following. By the time his book launched, he hit bestseller in seven categories. He'd been invited to guest blog and guest host in over a dozen outlets. His dream was to travel and be paid to speak in places where he could uplift people who'd been given a life-threatening diagnosis. Hospitals and health centers heard of him through the influencer posts. The week after his book launch, he was flown down to Mexico to speak at a wellness conference to over three thousand people.

BUILD

🙂 Your visibility expands exponentially, people know about you, your message is making a far greater impact

🙁 You don't have a powerhouse system to generate the sales and revenue to match all the incredible work you are doing

Writing + Speaking + Building an audience takes us incredibly far in our visions to impact the world. By using these first three strategies of the Thought Leader Pathway, you could find yourself on the plane to Mexico or doing an Instagram guest hosting gif on a major influencer's platform. But another challenge can arise at this point in the Thought Leader Pathway: income. Revenue. MONEY. We want more of it, need more, deserve more.

Even with major visibility, credibility and impact, unless we have powerful strategies in place to generate revenue, we can still end up underearning. With chagrin, I observed that there was still an element of the struggling coach/entrepreneur and the starving artist operating in me. And I knew I could only take our clients as far as I'd gone. My quest then became to learn the most authentic ways of the highest integrity to monetize the mission. I spent the next two years taking our business to multiple seven figures and reverse engineering a roadmap for all our thought leaders to do the same.

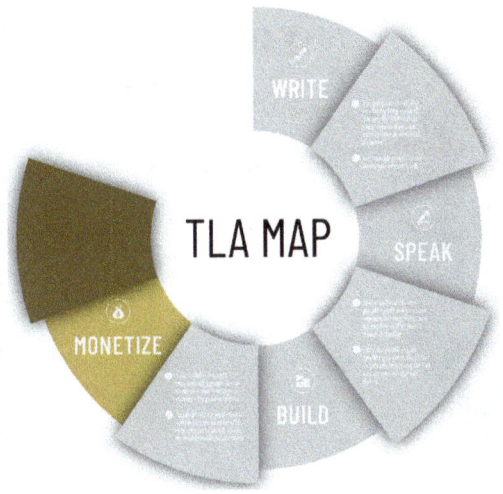

MONETIZE

🙂 NOW you're making the impact and income you desire and deserve and there are no limits 6-figures, 7 figures and beyond

🙁 Imposter syndrome, new challenges in building a team, scaling, systems- what got you here won't get you to the next level

Now, with all four strategies of the Thought Leader Pathway in play, you are cooking with fire.

The fifth and final strategy in the pathway is LEAD, which is about MINDSET, developing the leadership and identity that allows us to go all the way to peak potential. At each new or bigger step forward, our brain will send up alarm bells. Imposter Syndrome will scream, "you're not enough! Who do you think you are?!" Without illuminated leadership, without support, you will be tempted to run back to the familiar, to stay in your lane, to fly below the radar. This is why we have an entire strategy devoted to your empowerment, your courage, your commitment to the vision. Fear can be formidable, but it is no match for the black belt mindset work you will do here, on the thought leader path. We're together now; I'm with you all the way.

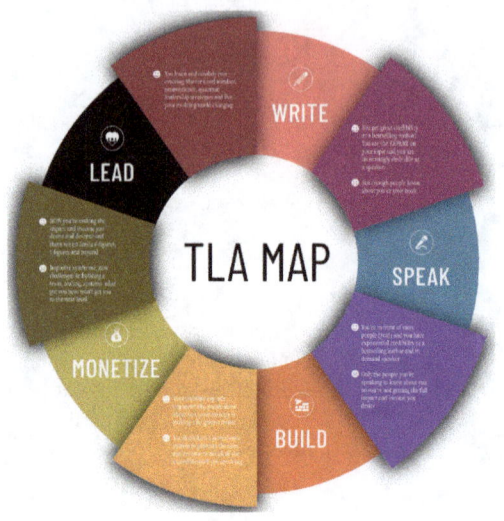

LEAD

🙂 You learn and embody ever evolving Master Level mindset, neuroscience, quantum leadership strategies and live your evolving world changing

The five strategy Thought Leader Pathway allows you to do in one year what it took me ten years to do. I'm SO excited to give you the roadmap, the secret tips, the fast-track through the forest. Let's GO!

CHAPTER TWO

Mind the Gap

In May 2014, *The Atlantic Monthly* ran an article by Katty Kay and Claire Shipman that sent ricochets of familiar rage and uncomfortable recognition through many women in America. First the article summarized that while women now obtained more college and graduate degrees than men, made up over half the workforce, and outperformed men in contribution and profitability, studies by both Goldman Sachs and Columbia University found that men continued to be promoted faster and paid more than their equally talented and qualified female colleagues. That was the familiar rage part. The wage gap between men and women was probably already happening when the prehistoric man Gargon got more for his cave painting than his wife Geela in the caves of Lascaux, through when we traded shells as currency, right up to what we see now in our post-pandemic Fortune 1000 companies where women make $0.83 to the male dollar and women of color make an unconscionable $0.65.

The uncomfortable recognition came in the article's revelation: that one REASON women may be continuing to earn less, be promoted less, was not *only* due to patriarchal biases within companies, but that women didn't believe they DESERVED to earn more. Women, the article showed us, were suffering from something called The Confidence Gap, a phenomenon whereby women underestimated their skill, performance and worth by about 25 percent. Men overestimated by about 30 percent, so our society was operating in about a 50 percent confidence gap, and, according to the article, it was hurting us. Success (income, contribution, influence, achievement, leadership opportunities), it turns out, is determined by confidence just as much as competence.

Suddenly, instead of only the numbing rage of the unfairness of the inequity of pay, we were faced with some new knowledge, that at last partly "the call was coming from inside the house."

If you've traveled to London, you'll have heard the Tube (subway) conductor's warning to passengers to "mind the gap," to take precautions not to fall into the deep space between the station platform and the train when boarding. As women leaders, the confidence gap is one we must "mind" and transcend in order to contribute and transform our world.

Here's a familiar scenario. Three friends, two female, one male, take a college class together. After the midterm, they agree to meet outside to discuss. The women gather first and admit to feeling a churning in their stomachs. "I don't know," they worry. "I prepared, I know this stuff, but I'm not sure how I did. I probably bombed." Their male friend enters a minute later. "Killed it!" he says, grinning. They all did well on the test. Fast forward and this same group is experiencing the same dynamic as realtors or lawyers or doctors or in the C-suites of large companies. The women worry constantly that they're not enough and the men continue to believe they are "killing it."

Without question, a REASON so many women doubt themselves is because of centuries of racial and gender programming of our inferiority. AND wherever the cause originated, as much as I hated to admit it, I related to the "dark something," the imposter syndrome thoughts, the stomach plunge after taking a risk, the fear I had done badly, lashing myself with what I should've done better, plaguing self-doubt and fear, I wasn't or wouldn't be good enough or capable of the next big goal. I was the women in that article. Do you relate?

If you'll give me just another beat on the confidence gap (I promise, I'll get to strategies on thought leadership soon), evidence emerged a few years after *The Atlantic* article when a Freshbooks study demonstrated that women freelancers (who set their own rates and work for themselves) made 28 percent less on average than equal male counterparts. WHY? When people interviewed women freelancers, they discovered that the earnings gap was due, in part, to the women freelancer's difficulty charging what they were worth, raising rates, and pitching bigger projects. And again, when VIDA (an organization that aims to create accountability in publishing by distributing stats on who publishers choose to feature each year), called out magazine editors for publishing far more white men than any other group. One male editor, instead of mumbling an apology, or promise to "do better," courageously offered some feedback. From what I recall (and this is my paraphrase), the editor said he'd love to publish more women in his magazine. The women, though, he said, weren't submitting the same amount of work.

Women submit less than half the volume of men. When I reject a piece of writing from a man, but ask him to send me more articles or stories, he does. When I give the same offer to women, almost none of them send me anything else. I rarely hear from them again.

When I read the VIDA information, I was called to look at my own behavior. How many times had I submitted a piece of writing and if it received even one rejection, trashed it, thinking, "I guess it isn't good." This is a terrible publishing strategy. It wasn't until I met a mentor at Northwestern, who told me anytime she receives a rejection, she sends out three more writing pieces to other publications, and read the game-changing Lit Hub piece about a women actively "going after" one hundred rejections that I broke through my confidence gap and started doing one hundred submissions (minimum) for every writing piece. Probably not a surprise, that Power 100 strategy I now use and teach to our clients in Thought Leader Academy took me from unpublished to having every piece of writing I've submitted for publication being published. EVERY ONE.

Whether you read *The Atlantic* article or not, whether you identify as female, male, non-binary, the Confidence Gap is real, and if you weren't raised and conditioned by your family, culture, religion, society, and ancestry to think you're amazing, this gap may be affecting your progress, legacy, and success. In this book, we're going to change that.

Before I show you how to overcome, even smash that gap, a quick note about why confidence is important. Confidence is linked staggeringly to the action we will take and the ability to enroll others in supporting, investing in, promoting, partnering, and hiring us.

Importantly, a lack of confidence (appearing in the form of self-doubt, fear of judgment and rejection, imposter syndrome, business dysmorphia, and the lingering effects of childhood and ancestral trauma), is the number one reason YOU and millions of other amazing, heart-centered, mission-driven individuals like you have not already reached the full potential of your leadership, contribution, and legacy. We think it's time and money, but we will always find the time or the money for what we believe matters vitally.

This could seem grim. The majority of women in America live in this gap and have to transcend it in order to succeed?

The great news is there is a faster solution than waiting until we develop confidence and close the confidence gap. There is a way to hack the system and move into confidence-level results, without feeling confident at all. The remedy to the CG predicament is: AUDACIOUS ACTION.

What happens currently, as we've already explored, is that:

Lack of Confidence=negative thoughts=fear/doubt/shame etc.=playing small/avoiding action toward vision=small results.

Trying to heal all the cultural, ancestral, religious, familial barriers to our confidence may take some time, so instead of waiting until we do ten years of therapy, we make the engine the caboose.

Regardless of lack-centered thoughts/feelings, we take *Audacious Action*. The action feels audacious because we're flying in the face of all those scary imposter syndrome messages.

In the face of "no one will publish you," you go send your work to one hundred publications.

In the cackle of "no one cares what you have to say," you make one hundred Instagram lives and start to engage a wide audience.

In the drone of "people will reject you/no one wants what you're offering," you make an invitation a day for people to hire you and work with you, and you start actually earning income and transforming lives.

Dan Sullivan, the founder of Strategic Coach, a global organization that trains thousands of entrepreneurs per year, wrote a book called *The 4 C's*, which emphasizes the power of Audacious Action. Dan says movement happens in the reverse order of what most people desire. They want confidence first, but Dan says it goes like this: Commit + Courage + Competence leads to Confidence. The feisty, honest thought leader Mel

Robbins affirms this premise as well, saying "confidence is NOT a feeling, but rather a STATE achieved through taking courageous action."

I'm inviting you to take Audacious Action with me for the rest of this book and hopefully for the rest of your life. I believe this is the fastest way we can heal and eradicate the confidence gap for ourselves and excitingly for everyone around us! When you are audacious and courageous, you give others permission to be courageous. When you play big, you give everyone a bridge to their next big leap. In the movie, *The Moses Code*, Michael Beckwith says, "God doesn't call the qualified, he qualifies the called." You can translate that to life/the universe doesn't single out "qualified/special/talented" people, it supports, prospers, and actualizes those who take action on a vision. You don't need confidence to manifest the greatness inside you. You just need to GO!

In order to be laser clear on where we are going, what these audacious actions should be, we want a laser clear VISION.

Let's play a game. If you waved a magic wand and suddenly you were doing all you dreamed of contributing to the world, where you are making the full impact and income you desire to make, when you have created the legacy you feel pulsing in your heart, what is happening?

At our Thought Leader retreats, we call this your Future Bio. Author Cameron Harold calls it your Vivid Vision.

Imagine you are being interviewed by your favorite podcast host (the one you secretly picture yourself on and would do naked cartwheels on the street when you booked it). Write the one paragraph introduction the host would read when introducing you to their audience. You know, the one where the hosts plugs your bestselling book, the Netflix documentary, your seven-figure business, the thousands of people you've helped. Write without censorship, write without fear, write without that judging, gremlin, logical, patriarchal voice that will tell you this is silly, a fantasy, that you'll never achieve it. Write faster than the gremlin can keep up with you.

Making the Vision a Reality

Just like in a car GPS, when we plug in our desired destination in order to get our roadmap, we also need to enter our current location. To customize your step-by-step actions to get you to that future bio, to make your Vivid Vision your present day reality, read through the following and identify where you land currently on the Thought Leader Pathway. Then you can take the thought leader assessment and find out your exact next steps at:

You'll also receive your Audacious Action next steps customized to get you to the next level!

MIND THE GAP

ASCENDING LEVELS OF A THOUGHT LEADER

INVISIBLE THOUGHT LEADER (Under $100K)

- You post content but very few people engage
- You work with a smaller group of clients than you'd like, often 1-1, and feel frustrated by few followers online
- You have few thought leader assets already created: ie book, signature talk, course
- You feel shame and frustration at the disparity between how hard you work and the money you're receiving
- At least once, you've found yourself NOT promoting a product, book, or course, even though you want everyone to buy it

EMERGING THOUGHT LEADER ($100K)

- You've developed more Mastery of your craft
- You're more confident in your mission, offers and work
- You may have started to work in groups vs 1-1
- You have at least 1 additional offer/way for people to work with you
- You're more visible for sure yet you're still getting less than 1/2 of the profits, engagement, referrals and visibility you want.
- You feel shame and frustration at the disparity between how hard you work and the money you're receiving.

THOUGHT LEADER ACADEMY

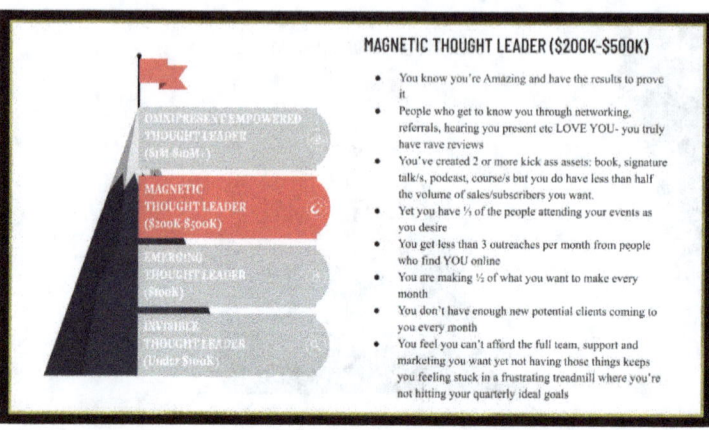

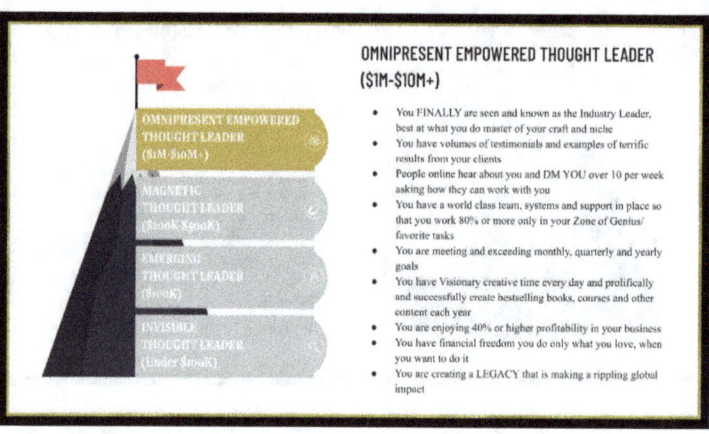

Add any insights from the thought leader assessment to your future bio/vision.

Now that you have a clearer picture of where you're going and the first Audacious Actions to take, we're going to pack a few more power tools for the journey.

CHAPTER THREE

Thought Leader Agreements

Four point six seconds.

That's the time I've heard it takes from moment of (divine) inspiration (I'm going to write a book, become a speaker, pitch podcasts, launch a course, become a seven-figure CEO!) to feeling besieged by thoughts and fears that we can't/won't/don't deserve/aren't capable. Has this happened to you?

Carl Jung called this the saboteur, psychologists call this the inner critic, Steven Pressfield in his wonderful book, *The War of Art*, calls this Resistance. In Thought Leader Academy, we call these fearful, often loud and pervasive beasties, "the gremlins."

Whatever they're called, experts from almost every tradition observe that there is a reaction in the human mind, when courage, passion, and motivation kick in, that pulls in an equal and opposite direction away from the growth, the expansion, the creativity, passion, and success. A part of us that wants only to stay safe, familiar, in the comfort zone, and will say or do anything it can to drag us back from making our next big leap.

Neuroscientists have identified a part of the brain involved in this reaction called the amygdala, and its job is to sound alarms and flashing lights of threat! Concern! Not safe! The minute we even contemplate doing something new, exciting, and brave.

Stepping into being a thought leader as a bestselling author, speaking on stages or giving interviews on podcasts, finding and leading the people you are here to serve, increasing your revenue and life abundance (if we aren't already doing these things or are planning to do them in a bigger way), are most certainly going to trigger our sweet amygdala into a panic!

So, a few years ago, I went in search of antidotes to the gremlins, to RESISTANCE, and will share them with you in this book. To get us started, we created five "thought leader agreements" that I use and our clients use in the Academy to shift our state from fear to empowerment, from defeat to victory, from stuck to unstoppable!

As you read through the five agreements, see if there's one that excites you or also if there's one you heartily dislike. Both responses contain information.

Thought Leader Agreement One:
Your desire is your destiny.

For years I would get up every day and ask for signs. I read and reread *The Alchemist*, a book whose central premise is "follow the omens." I wanted other people, life, nature, the universe to give me confidence, permission, reassurance that what I was about to do was a good idea, that it was supported, that I was on the right track.

I still love receiving signs. My entire chest tingles when, in the almost mystical experience of mulling over a challenge and then right there on the highway, my answer appears emblazoned in thirty-foot letters across a billboard.

(Actual billboard I drove by on the highway the day I asked if I should create a new program for Thought Leaders.)

I love it when the next step I need to take reveals itself in the form of a song on the radio or the words out of a podcast host's mouth or my son's friend who is quoting some book he just read. Asking for signs is a terrific thing. AND . . .

After walking my journey and coaching amazing individuals for the past two decades, I now believe that the desire itself, the initial spark, the calling to create or be or do something new and great IS the sign.

I believe we would not even desire something if that desire wasn't our destiny to have it. So this first agreement is essentially inviting you to trust yourself. To trust that life or God or your higher self or the universe wouldn't have had the desire to begin with if it wasn't available. If you weren't already approved, worthy, capable, and supported in doing it.

So if you've been asking for a sign, consider that you reading this paragraph right now is your moment of affirmation. Whatever vision had you pick up this book to begin with IS the sign that you're meant to do it!

Thought Leader Agreement Two: Fear (self-doubt, resistance, especially imposter syndrome) is an AFFIRMATION that we are on our soul's path.

Wait! What? We just discussed not needing signs to tell us we're on the right path, and here I am saying that fear and doubt and "who do you think you are?" are signs! Yes, that's what I'm saying. I'm offering a paradox, so thanks for sticking with me. Here's what I mean for agreement two. Remember our dear amygdala, that part of the brain tasked with freaking us the f— out anytime we attempt or think seriously about attempting something new? Well, the amygdala for all its clashing and banging and ferocious noise and bringing of waves of adrenaline and cortisol is not an enlightened part of us. It does not see what's on the other side of the uncomfortable, new feelings. It can't see that the very thing it's shouting at you not to do (DON'T GO DOWN IN THE BASEMENT) is the exact thing that will move you into the greater abundance, freedom, fulfillment, joy, success, and positive impact that you deeply desire. So instead of hearing those alarm bells and running back to the couch to watch Netflix and eat a carton of (insert your favorite snack), give yourself a huge high ten in the mirror, shimmy your shoulders back down off your ears, and say, "THANK YOU for letting me know it's GAME ON!"

Thought Leader Agreement Three: I am one with that.

Often, when we see someone do something that we've been longing to do: publish a bestselling book, launch a business, buy a new home, go on an incredible trip, have a baby, we feel separate. We try to be happy for the people, we even are happy for them. But we think maybe they had opportunities we didn't or that there's something's wrong with us or we don't deserve the great thing they've just created.

We might feel like we're just as good and capable, but it will never happen for us because it hasn't already and we can't see the HOW.

In this agreement, we flip the script. Instead of separating, we UNIFY. Every time you see someone doing something awesome that you also want to do, say I AM ONE WITH THAT.

You likely won't believe this at first. You'll say pst-shwa. This is a bunch of coaching (insert favorite swear word). Before you reject this, consider something I heard a neuroscientist say once. He explained that scientists used to think the brain received 60,000 thoughts a day. The number at the time of my writing this is 60,000 thoughts per *minute*, and many scientists think it's likely more. Because consciously processing this number of impressions would drive us into drooling madness, our brains (particularly the reticular activating system), filters out almost all of these thoughts. It's trying to do us a big favor, but in addition to helping us stay sane, it filters out the majority of ideas, impressions, possibilities, opportunities, and inspirations that are swimming all around us. The bottom line: we only see what the RAS thinks is relevant to our identity, so if you're seeing something that you want and don't yet have and you feel less than or angry or jealous, get excited! You wouldn't even SEE that thing if it wasn't part of your destiny.

At this point, I get excited to feel a stab of jealousy because I now believe jealousy is simply something we haven't let ourselves be that we are destined to be/do/have. I regard jealousy as a sneak preview of coming attractions.

Using I AM ONE WITH THAT dissolves jealousy and replaces it with excited anticipation. We can remind ourselves that there is only one life force flowing through everything and so therefore the same greatness that created whatever that other person achieved is the same force that lives in our cells, beats our hearts, thinks our thoughts.

Try I AM ONE WITH THAT for just a week. See what happens. You're on Instagram. And someone's just had a big million dollar launch and you say I AM ONE WITH THAT. Someone you know is standing on the TEDx stage in that red circle: I AM ONE WITH THAT. Someone posts a photo of their number one new release bestseller: I AM ONE WITH THAT.

And so it is.

Thought Leader Agreement Four: The answer is in the room.

Almost fifteen years ago, I was invited to speak at a conference where Marianne Williamson was speaking. She owned the stage and rousted the audience to their feet in a speech about the necessity to care for every child on the planet as our own biological child. What I remember even more than the standing ovation, the tremble in my chest as this tiny, fiery woman, the woman who'd spoken one of my favorite quotes ever spoken (you know the *"when we shine our light we give others permission to do that same so who are you to be talented, brilliant, successfully, fabulous? Who are you not to be?"* one), was something she said much earlier in her talk. It isn't recorded, but what I remember is her saying, in nature wherever a poisonous plant grows, the antidote can be found growing within twelve feet. I remember the context of this comment being about how life is all sufficient, of how well taken care we are by the universe.

My brain stuck on that idea. Turned it over and over for days afterwards. What I decided the twelve-feet phenomenon meant-metaphorically-is that whatever challenge arises, the solving idea, antidote, resource, support is at hand. It's growing within twelve feet. The answer we need is here. Extrapolated out a bit, THE ANSWER IS IN THE ROOM.

Now, when I lead groups in a virtual room, an in-person room, even a metaphorical "room" of a community, I walk in the belief that the answers we all need are present, already here, exist right where we are. When I share this agreement at the start of a workshop, a retreat, or a Thought Leader Academy Q&A, I invite the participants and our members to treat the session as an experiment. They think of a question or issue they're having and see, if by the end of our time together, the issue has been answered or solved. Often it has entirely or at minimum a next step and forward movement has been revealed.

Try THE ANSWER IS IN THE ROOM out as you read the rest of this book. Act as if whatever you need is here for you. Notice, even write down, how these revelations and solutions emerge and how often you didn't have to make an effort, but instead, by your choosing to play with the concept that THE ANSWER IS IN THE ROOM, you summoned and received.

Thought Leader Agreement Five: You can and you will.

Three years ago we had this phrase printed on little wooden signs and gave them to all the participants at a wedding, starting with a men's retreat.

Often we think of a big goal, we have a vision, something we really want to desire. We go into different energies around it at the lowest end, we think that's a fantasy. It's a pipe dream. It'll never happen for me. Kind of the Charlie Brown effect that maybe it's I wish it would happen. I hope it will happen. Try out each of these statements. Pick a goal that you have and try this out first. "I want to write a bestselling book, but it will probably never happen for me." See what happens in your body, your energy, your emotions. Now shake that off and try on, "I hope I write a bestselling book." Same thing. What's your posture? What are the emotions you're feeling? Like the setup, a little straighter, you felt a little bit of a chest expansion. Now try on, "I can write a bestselling book."

Maybe you feel like you grew an edge or you took a deep, parasympathetic breath, and now, "I will write a bestselling book."

You could take it a step further. "I am a bestselling author." Each of these statements will produce a different physiological energetic and emotional state. You can and you will. It's so exciting. We're on Zoom calls with Thought Leader Academy. Sometimes we unmute and share this to a member who's ready to take a big leap. You can and you will. It's so much fun to think of things we desire and bolster our cell phones like this. You can and you will. I recommend writing that up somewhere and sticking it where you can see it or you're going to sit down to do your emails or start your book or pitch that next talk. Whatever you desire, follow it up with, I can and I will, and you will.

CHAPTER FOUR

Thought Leader Pathway Strategy One: Lead

YOUR STORY DETERMINES YOUR REALITY

As I mentioned previously, the first crucial step in becoming the free, empowered thought leader you are here to be is to POWERFULLY LEAD YOUR OWN THOUGHTS. In the coming chapters, I will teach you how to write a bestselling book, how to share your story, methods, and genius in a way that can change minds and lives and scale your vision to six or seven figures. But first, we must ensure your internal stories are aligned with your thought leader vision.

You've likely heard your thoughts create beliefs and beliefs determine the actions we take. I call these beliefs: STORIES. We are all running personal stories (often on a subconscious level). Remember my first experience with the literary agent? I had a story that I wasn't good enough and she would be the one to ultimately seal my fate. Because of this "not good enough story," I couldn't write. These invisible stories have the power to fulfill our thought leader destiny, or have us end our life unfulfilled, with our music still buried inside us.

We can easily find out what kind of story we are running by looking at the results of our current life. The amount of money we have and how we feel about that money is a result of our story. Our relationship status and quality= story. Our health= the story our minds tell our bodies. Our visibility and success in the world, story.

And if you're tempted to skip this section and jump straight to how to write and publish your bestselling, thought leader book, I urge you to stay here and keep reading because the power of the story we are running is gobsmacking.

In 2007, Harvard conducted a study with eighty-four female hotel cleaners working in seven different hotels. The control group was told nothing. The second group was told that the work they did clearing hotel rooms satisfied the Surgeon General's recommendations for exercise. The cleaners were given examples and data of how the work they did: vacuuming, changing bedsheets, scrubbing bathtubs, etc., was equivalent of someone doing a workout. Both groups went about their work as usual, making no changes to lifestyle or routine. After four weeks, the women in the group who were told (a story), that their work was real exercise, showed a decrease in weight, blood pressure, body fat, waist-to-hip ratio, and body mass index. The control group had no change in any of these physical states.

How could this be? None of the women changed their activities! Yet the group who was told the exercise story lost weight! People doing the same amount of movement, eating the same amount of food, should have the same health results. But they didn't! The STORY the women believed about themselves and their health trumped the actual biological reality. The STORY created the result.

You can read more about the study here:
https://dash.harvard.edu/bitstream/handle/1/3196007/langer_excersiseplaceboeffect.pdf?sequence=1

In Ben Hardy's book, *Be Your Future Self Now*, he shares the results of a Boyd and MacNeil study done with second and third grade students in a classroom. A group of researchers privately told teachers which students were gifted and which ones weren't based on an IQ test they'd administered. The teachers behaved accordingly, expecting more of the gifted students, giving them more challenging work, and expected less and challenged less the "average" students. As everyone in the study expected, at the end of the year, the gifted students showed "extremely higher" increases in learning and overall development than the "non-gifted" students. But here's the thing. The researchers had never administered the IQ tests. They randomly chose which students to tell the teachers were gifted and which weren't. The student's natural intelligence and ability did not determine their results. The STORY that the teachers held about them and transmitted through tangible and intangible signals to the students determined the results.

During my masters work at Northwestern, one of my professors told me about a teacher who tried a different kind of experiment. She was given a report about her incoming students for the school year. She was given data (report card grades, test scores) that a certain group of students was remedial, performing at least two grades below grade level. These were kids who could feel that their educators had, to an extent, given up on them.

This teacher gave a mock test at the beginning of the year. She took the remedial students aside and told them they'd scored "gifted" on a new test. She called their group the "gifted" throughout the year and gave them challenging work. These were kids reading two levels below their grade and who'd been told repeatedly that they were stupid. They didn't believe her at first, but the teacher insisted. The new test proved they had scored highest in the class. For a full year, she worked the gifted group, and by the last day of school, they were scoring a grade ahead of the national average. Same kids, same intelligence, same abilities. The new STORY gave them a new identity. The STORY determined their destiny.

Before I'd read or heard of any of these studies, I had my own experience with a story ruling my life. In sixth grade, I transferred from Catholic school into a public school in my neighborhood. All new students were given an assessment with a district psychiatrist. Dr. Allan looked like all the male administrators at the school. He wore brown trousers and a tan short sleeve, button-down shirt. Midway through the exam, he put down his silver wire-rimmed glasses and said, "My God! I've never seen anything like this. When did you find out you have a severe learning disability?"

I was stunned. I'd always gotten *A*s in school and had never even heard the term learning disability let alone that I had one. I was admitted into the "gifted" program with the exception of math where he told me I would struggle (along with reading maps, spatial relations, standardized tests, and anything to do with numbers), and I went from a confident front row student in all subjects to hiding in the back of math class, feeling embarrassed that there was something wrong with my brain. Guess what happened? Yep. Despite getting *A*s and thriving in other subjects, I struggled with standardized tests, spatial relations, reading maps, earning money (those pesky numbers). That is until I moved to England and started reading about neuroscience and quantum physics and the idea that our thoughts create our reality. I entered a program in holistic medicine that required a science exam with equations. I decided to see if I created a new story, if I could free myself from Dr. Allan's pronouncement. I thought back to the years before sixth grade and that test. My brain had been so creative to find "workarounds" for its "deficiencies" that neither I or my parents or teachers ever knew it was "abnormal." I started in on my science coursework repeating "I am great at science and math. Numbers come easily to me. My brain works perfectly. I have a super brain."

I scored the highest in the region on the exam.

As much as I wish none of us had Dr. Allan's in our life who feed us limiting stories about our worth and capability, many of us do. The exciting truth is that because of neuroplasticity (the brain's ability to grow and evolve), we can (and I will say MUST), swap out the limiting stories that do not align with our vision and destiny for new stories that empower, support, and actually go to work subconsciously to fulfill every one of our dreams.

We can revise ANY belief, no matter how potent and how long we've had it. In the first thought leader strategy, we do this work. We do it as much and as many times as we need to in order to align every part of ourselves, body, mind, and spirit with our thought leader vision.

Now it's your turn.

Take an area of your life that you wish was different- something that is not yet fully aligned with your vision. You can do this exercise on your own, or go to the Thought Leader Workbook and I'll guide you through it.

1. On a piece of paper or fresh screen, write the area of your life and the result you're currently experiencing.
2. Then ask yourself, "What story would someone be running to create this result?" and write whatever comes to you.

Example: Finances

Current result: Making $60K a year when I want to be making $600K/year.

The story that could create that result is: I'm not capable of earning multiple six figures.

OR

I'm not worthy of earning $600K/year.

OR

It's bad to care about money.

OR

People who make that kind of money are greedy/selfish.

OR

Other people can earn a lot of money, but I can't.

OR

There's something wrong with me.

OR

I can't earn more than my ___ (sister, Dad, Mom, friends).

Or on and on.

Keep exploring possible stories until something "zings." Many different stories could create that result, but you'll know when it's a story you're running because you'll feel a response in your body. It will hurt a little to read it out loud.

Now to a much more fun part of the process.

3. Write the story that someone would believe to create the result you DO want. I.e.

When I make more money, everyone wins.

It's easy for me to make multiple six figures/year through work I love.

It's fun and authentic to me to make tons of money.

Starting today, I'm great at earning money. I'm wildly, crazy, super abundant now.

You get the idea. Write a bunch of options and just like with the old, limiting story, play around until you find one that uplifts you. The one that if it were true would bring you joy and have you jump up out of bed in the morning excited to take on the day.

Now PRETEND that you've been put under a wonderful spell and the new story you've chosen is activated in every cell of your body. Walk around thinking, feeling, and acting as if it's true. Make decisions today based on that new story. Let people close to you who are committed to empowering you know the new story. Invite them to see you and engage with you based on the new narrative. Refuse to engage in any old talk with the limiting story. The limiting story had plenty of air time and you're up to big things and need a new story to get you there.

Finally, every day, write down evidence of the new story becoming your reality. Borrow from others at first if you need. Notice everyone

THOUGHT LEADER PATHWAY STRATEGY ONE: LEAD

who is already living what you want to live as proof that it's possible for you too. Say, "I am one with that!" Like the person working on abundance who celebrates every dime they find on the street on their way to receiving millions, you now make it your mission to notice every single piece of proof that you are lovable, successful, worthy, capable, supported, destined, and that your thought leader vision is your reality NOW! You want to go all the way to having your new story be your reality? Take AUDACIOUS, ALIGNED ACTION based on your new story and watch the old story go up in a blaze.

The year I first made one million dollars, I let go of the story that I was bad with money, that I wasn't capable of running a seven-figure business, and that other people could make a million dollars in a year, but I couldn't. My new story was: I AM A SEVEN-FIGURE CEO. I wouldn't have smashed my glass ceiling if I'd just thought about making a million dollars. But running the new story every morning when I got up, seeing myself in the mirror as a seven-figure CEO, and then ACTING as a seven-figure CEO (expanding my team, writing two books, speaking on bigger stages, and creating new and better content in Thought Leader Academy), took me the rest of the way.

Your rational mind will fight you (and me!) on this. It will tell you this STORY swapping is some make-believe, reality denying nonsense. Your gremlins will remind you all the times you've tried to change or done personal growth or law of attraction techniques and it hasn't "worked." Do it anyway and that skeptical part will stand with its mouth open as you open your bank account, stand on the stage holding your book, receive that industry expert award, and hardly keep up with the THANK YOU emails in your inbox.

* * *

One of our first Thought Leader Academy clients came in with a limiting story. She'd developed a simple, powerful, and creative way for people to access their intuition and identify their soul's purpose. She received such powerful guidance for people that they often had instant and permanent shifts and healings just from talking to her. When she spoke, she often used beautiful, lyrical descriptions, and I could easily see that she would write a powerful, beautiful book.

But when she was four, she'd given her father a handmade birthday card. He took out a red pen and showed her all the spelling and grammar mistakes she'd made. "You're not much of a writer," he said. She was FOUR! Instead of understanding that her father was likely a perfectionist and brutally hard on himself and therefore her, she made up a story. "I'm a bad writer."

So decades later, when she felt called to thought leadership, she balked at the book step. I kept encouraging her to write. We did all kinds of workarounds to help her brain feel safe putting words on the page. Writing at first was a challenge. The old story screamed in her ear. But she started living from a new story: I am a talented, gifted writer who has an important message to share with the world. It took some time, but she finished that book. It became an instant bestseller. She's been asked to speak in front of hundreds of people based on that book. It's been translated into other languages. Last year, we stood together in Times Square, New York City and her book cover flashed onto the screen, stunning, strong, a blaze of intuition blue. We held hands and cried as someone in the crowd that had assembled said, "That looks good; who's that book by?" and she got to say, "Me."

* * *

From this day forward, YOU are the author of your story. And now that you've claimed a powerful story aligned with your thought leader vision, you're ready to WRITE the story you're here to share, the one that's going to change the world.

CHAPTER FIVE

Write

When a totalitarian government takes power, the first people they lock up are the writers.

In 2017, I attended an event in the West Loop in Chicago. The event was part of a series called Writer's Resist, which was created following the 2016 US presidential election. The featured speaker that evening was an award-winning, "famous" writer I admired. She shared that she had recently traveled to Russia, and while there, she met a female writer from Moscow who told her she'd been imprisoned twice and that a colleague of hers had been killed, by the government. In a very flat, matter-of-fact way, the Russian writer added, "The first people they arrest are the writers."

Why would the writers be the first ones rounded up off the streets?

Because writing and story are the vehicles for transmitting the most powerful ideas and information since the oral histories of cultures were created.

You've already heard about the book that saved my life. I've never met Margaret Bullitt-Jonas, yet her book saved my life. Imagine your book like some supersonic life raft you can toss not just to one, but to millions of readers, all at once.

A part of you will doubt the value of your idea and try to seduce you into thinking no one will read what you write anyway, but another part of you knows there's a person out there or hundreds of someone's or thousands of someone's or even millions of someone's, asking, praying, calling in the message only you can share.

You have your divine ideas. You have your unique way of seeing things and doing things. And it's part of this incredible cosmic puzzle. That's gonna help everybody win, including you, so what's the first step? So many people come to me and say, I know I have a book in me, but what do I write? How do I write it and how do we get it published? And how do we get it out to people? There are so many steps. It's easy to talk ourselves out of this talk versus off the mountain for you to reach the first base camp. We forget, depending on where we live in the world, we are likely free to write whatever we wish and what a privilege that is, and we forget what the book can open up in our lives, its ability to impact, and our success. We talked about the life-changing potential of your book AND there are gifts for you too. Because of writing books, I have spoken on stages in front of a thousand people, I have presented at TEDx, I've been on every major television network, in top magazines, won awards, and been able to contribute to independent bookstores and organizations and events I care about and love. I've made millions of dollars. Last week, I was in Paris, meeting readers from other continents, giving a reading of my newest book while the Eiffel Tour glimmered against the skyline.

I want all this for you. I want you to impact people in a massive way, and I want you to be invited to speak on amazing stages and travel the world and attract incredible people to work with you and make huge amounts of money. So, I'm going to show you a process. A process I hope makes the idea of getting your writing done and into the world easier. You can apply this process to any type of writing and any length-from emails to a three hundred page memoir. You don't have to discover fire or invent the printing press. Writing a whole book can be accomplished by taking the next step.

Step One: The Whiteboard

One of the first challenges that the leaders, coaches, and experts I coach have starts before they even begin writing: how to choose the ONE idea or topic for their book. Visionaries rarely have just one book idea; they have five.

Right now, ask yourself, how many book ideas do you have? Two? Seven? One client arrived to her first session with twelve book ideas. A vegan cookbook, a memoir about her grandmother's immigration to the United States from Serbia, the games she made up to play in the car with her kids when it was her weekend with them, oh and yeah, the book about her business . . .

I help up my hands. "How much have you written of each of these?" I asked her.

"Nothing," she said. "I just swirl from idea to idea."

I understood completely. Currently, there are seven books I want to write. On any given month, I have between three and ten book ideas. Like my client though, until I choose one, and go all in with that idea, one at a time, I never do what we call in Thought Leader Academy "launch the rocket."

If you already have your ONE idea, you are welcome to skip to the next section. If you are in a book topic swirl, you can go through this technique here in the book, or I can walk you through the entire WRITE process virtually:

What I did that day with my client with the twelve book ideas was pull out my whiteboard. I gave her ten different dry erase markers in fun, bright colors and had her write every idea on the board. Then I took her through the prompts I use with our thought leaders to let the ONE idea rise, shining and sparkling to the surface. Let's do it together. Write all your awesome book (or article, blog, etc.), ideas on your whiteboard or a fresh computer screen.

Then, Eliminate any "shoulds." (Everyone says I should write about my experience backpacking through India, but I don't really want to.)

Next, circle or highlight the book ideas that align with these questions:

Which book am I most excited to write?

If I could only write one book as my legacy, which of these would it be?

What is my most important goal this year, and which book most closely aligns with it?

What are my ideal book outcomes? (Inspiring/educating? Speaking? Attracting clients? Being seen as an industry expert?)

This series of questions often brings the clarity we seek. You may have multiple ideas that light you up and would be an amazing legacy, but typically one of your ideas most aligns with your most important overall goal and the outcomes you desire. If you want to be paid to speak and be seen as an industry expert in functional medicine, but you have this idea for a memoir about living in LA in your twenties, a thought leader book about holistic health is going to fulfill your overall vision far more than the memoir.

A few years ago, my number one goal was to grow in mastery of the craft of writing. That year, after doing the whiteboard, I wrote my short story collection, *Ghost House*. Often, fiction requires a higher level of craft work so that was the book that most required me to improve my craft. Last year, my number one goal was to empower our clients and women worldwide to monetize their missions. I was invited to write a novel and two nonfiction books, but I chose to write *The Science of Getting Rich for Women* so I could share our Thought Leader Academy monetize strategies with women in many countries around the globe.

When we choose our book topic based on our most important goal, the rewards are tremendous. The goal alignment creates synergy and momentum with all your endeavors. *The Science of Getting Rich for Women* became an interactive movement. We created a book portal with interactive resources so readers had more support in implementing the strategies. I created a free workbook. I created demos of the techniques. I recorded videos of the guided visualizations and exercises, and I interviewed twenty-five other self-made women millionaires so that many different voices and backgrounds are represented for people who read the book and get to know these women on the portal.

Do you have your ONE idea? If so, circle, highlight, star, and celebrate it! If you're not certain yet, fear not! Pick the lead idea from your whiteboard and keep going through the steps. I've never had a single person leave my Bestselling Book Intensive, where I take our clients through what I'm including in this chapter, and not get clear.

Step Two: Your *Bestselling* Book Idea

I love Venn diagrams! All those overlapping circles and ellipses. Such fun to see where various ideas and topics come together to create something bigger than the sum of their parts. To help our Thought Leader clients start to set up their book ideas as bestsellers before they start writing, I created this bestselling book Venn diagram that we will now use to confirm and further hone your book idea.

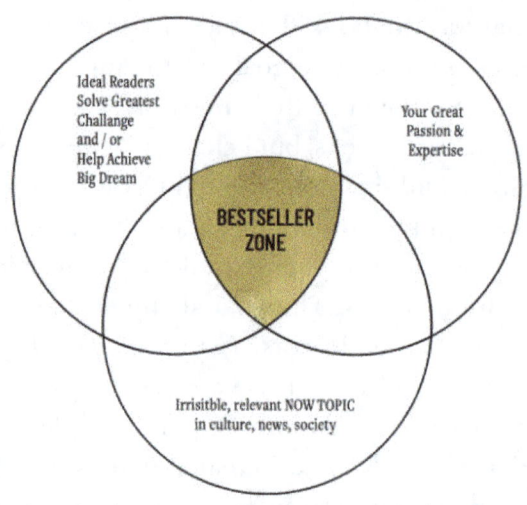

Remember you can download the worksheet for this section or go through all the steps with me here:

In the upper right circle, we have your passion and expertise. Expertise can come in many forms. Some people get freaked out at this one because they think, I don't have a PhD; I didn't even go to college. Doesn't matter. Your passion and expertise can be based on your lived experience. Or work you've done with others. A really cool revelation that you've had. In order to stick with a book, you want to feel high passion, obsession even, for your topic. So circle one is about something you could think, talk, and write about for years and not get bored, combined with a topic with which you have some level of experience or expertise. What we're talking about here is the Shero or Hero's journey. Our leader (YOU) are called to a quest. You face challenges and obstacles. You triumph/learn some things and bring what you've learned back to the community. That's circle number one.

Now the top left circle. What we're looking for here is how your book does one or both of these:

Help reader overcome a challenge or

Help reader achieve a dream.

The category of bestseller is based solely on numbers. How many books are sold. For something to be a bestseller, people have to read it and likely tell other people to read it too. Readers hound their friends, buy it for their mothers, choose the book for their book club. Now, before your gremlins go berserk and tell you how inept you will be at accomplishing circle number two, remember that a great book doesn't need to solve the WHOLE challenge or help someone achieve the ENTIRE dream. Just a single, powerful step can be more than enough. In Tim Ferris' book, *The 4 Hour Workweek*, the challenge he's addressing for entrepreneurs is overwhelm and lack of productivity and freedom. The specific focus of that book is how to drastically cut down time spent in meetings. He hasn't solved every issue of hiring, distribution, marketing, sales in a business, but he offers a compelling vision for freedom and gives some very specific strategies to get hours a week of your time back. Ferris' book was a HUGE bestseller and I doubt anyone complained to Tim Ferris that he didn't solve every challenge on their list.

It can also be helpful to remember that you being a fifth grader to someone else's third grader is a massive gift. You don't need to have graduated from MIT to be able to show someone how to create a great app, for example. Often, readers feel more comfortable learning from a guide a bit closer to their situation. It can be inspiring to read about a billionaire entrepreneur and his private island, but that can also feel like such a big gap, readers don't believe they can cross it. If you're a few steps ahead of your reader in something and offer them a way to join you at their next level, they'll read.

Circle two applies to fiction, poetry, and all genres of writing too. What's the challenge or the dream of someone who's reaching for a fantasy romance? Or a psychological or political thriller? Well, one thing is they might be really annoyed at what's happening in their actual life. And they want to be swept up, they want a distraction, they want an escape, they want to be lifted, or maybe they want to learn about another culture. Maybe they've been raised in a very homogenous area and they haven't had the opportunity to travel to a country where you've been or visited and want to travel there vicariously through you.

Every book can help solve a problem or help a reader achieve a next step toward a goal or dream.

Write how your idea can fulfill circle two now.

Circle number three: Urgency

This part of setting a book up as a bestseller is the most often overlooked. Exploring this circle will prepare you to have a book that will not only be a bestseller, but will have podcasts, magazines, and other media wanting you on their shows and in their pages. The objective of circle three is: what makes your idea relevant, important, and needed NOW.

Our TLA clients sometimes balk at this circle too. Likely your book topic is what's called "evergreen," meaning the topic is timeless. It will always be important to many readers to be a good parent, to earn more money, to spiritually evolve, and create health. AND, to set your book up as a bestseller, you'll want to find a "hook" to things happening in the world in the current moment that give the readers urgency. I think about Gary Chapman's book, *The Five Love Languages*. The book helps readers identify and understand their own top love language as well as those of the important people in their lives. Loving others the way THEY want to be loved vs how we like to receive love can transform marriages, work relationships, and parent-child dynamics. It's a fabulous book. I thought Gary could've become a gigantic bestseller all over again if he'd released that book again during the pandemic. The top two Venn diagram circles would have been the same. But the third circle would have started to zing. The urgency was now families, couples were stripped of their distractions, external environments, and were going to be holed up together for indefinite periods of time under high-stress conditions. The urgency was that the pandemic could make or break your relationship and his book would help ensure the relationship made it!

To discover what's relevant/urgent about your book topic, open up any social media platform and scan the news headlines. You'll see what people are complaining about and asking for help with on your topic. You can build circle three with studies, statistics, trends, new stories, or do your own social media poll. When you're able to convey your passion, easily explain how your book helps readers, and why it's relevant now, you'll attract readers and people/outlets with big audiences to share your book.

Step Three: The Category

Once you have your book topic, you get to decide what kind of book you are writing. Here are some of the main categories (aka genres), writers use to create inspiration and change in the world. I'll give you a quick synopsis of each so you can decide (like your book topic), which is ideal for your book.

Memoir: A memoir is written like a novel except it happens to be true. This type of book is where you share your personal story. And the book follows some kind of what's called an arc. So there'd be an inciting incident. Something really important with high stakes that you as the Shero of our story wants, the journey you took to try to get it, the climactic moment, did you get it or not? And then what's called the resolution or denouement.

A memoir is a powerful way to transform others through your personal story. It requires fairly heavy lifting from the writing craft perspective because you're going to write primarily in scenes and have a strong narrative engine that keeps the reader turning pages from start to finish. My first book that I published is a memoir called *Bringing in Finn*. It tells the seven-year story, the journey, my husband and I took from the day we started trying to have a family to my son's birth. The climax is the moment my son was born in an extraordinary way through my sixty-one-year-old mother as a surrogate. Yeah, that's true. Super Grandma.

The book starts with the moment we realize we might have a fertility problem, flashes back to some childhood trauma that likely led to those fertility issues, and goes through our arduous journey. Through miscarriage, stillborn twins, emptying our bank accounts for eight rounds of IVF. And then the wild, crazy, miraculous moment when my mother had the vision to offer to help. It's like science fiction, but it actually happened. Memoir is not autobiography, where you'd start with your birth and move forward chronologically. Instead, most often the story covers a certain period of time as in Elizabeth's Gilbert's, *Eat Pray Love*, or *The Glass Castle* by Jeanette Walls. For a nontraditional memoir structure, check out Glennon Doyle's excellent memoir, *Untamed* (a series of linked "essays" on her topic). You can do a memoir around healing a health crisis. Transforming a relationship. Pursuing a professional or personal goal. There are even subcategories of memoirs like food memoirs, travel memoirs, health memoirs, etc. What feeling do you have to each of these categories as you go through and decide which one resonates most for you in your book.

Book outcomes are important here. A memoir is ideal when your main goal is inspiration or education. You have an incredible story that you know needs to be shared. In my experience, memoir is not the ideal genre, if you want to use your book as a lead generator, a high-converting client attractor, or revenue generator in and of itself, beyond book sales. Although you can do some of these things in creative ways, if you feel most called to memoir the way Diane Wilson, one of our Thought Leader Academy members, did. Diane began a career in neuroscience after experiencing a traumatic brain injury. Although she wanted to grow her practice, speak at conferences, and help exponentially more people, she wanted to use her story, versus personal growth, as the vehicle. Diane has presented at Harvard, launched a podcast, won book awards, and attracted new clients, so I share this to say-go with your gut!

Novel: Novels follow that same S/Hero's Journey arc with an inciting incident, a deep desire of a main character, a quest with lots of challenges, a climactic moment, and a resolution. It just happens to be made up. You can create massive transformation and world change with novels as well as nonfiction. Think of *To Kill a Mockingbird*, or Toni Morrison's, *Beloved*. If you're going to do a novel, your main book outcomes will be to inspire, educate, create a world, or develop a brand as a writer in and of itself. You'll also want to know you're setting yourself up for extra work on craft and revisions. Because of all the world building and needing to come up with the story, purely out of imagination, all right, both fiction and nonfiction and love them both. If you're feeling called to this, go for it!!

Personal Growth: In a personal growth book, you are guiding the reader as a coach and their way through a process. Personal growth books are fantastic when you have an expertise, a methodology, a framework, a roadmap, a blueprint, or a program you want to take the reader through. In the personal growth category, you are coaching and guiding your reader. You may weave in your personal story, but the main objective is to move them through strategies and actions to achieve their desired result or transformation.

The Thought Leader: This is not an official book genre, but I created this category for our clients. If your main book outcomes are inspiration, lead generation, attracting awesome, ideal clients, making tons of money with your book, and having as much of this as possible, happen automatically, magnetically, I recommend this highly.

The thought leader book brings an exciting idea or perspective to your reader (think Malcolm Gladwell's, *Tipping Point,* or Marie Kondo's,

The Life-Changing Magic of Tidying Up), while weaving in your story, stories of people you've helped, and a signature system, process, roadmap to help your reader transform. The thought leader book is a combination of personal growth, self-help, and business leadership, and it's the kind of book that has produced the biggest results and multiple outcomes for our clients. The thought leader book is fantastic for establishing yourself as an industry expert. In the next section, I'll teach you a powerful structure for writing a bestselling thought leader book.

First though, sometimes the idea of choosing your category or genre can feel overwhelming, can bring you back into a swirl. What I know, after coaching leaders on books for over a decade, is that your book is already inside you. The content already exists. I don't mean only in a metaphysical, connected-to-the-universe kind of way (although that is true). I mean, you likely have terrific book content at hand. If you have a coaching program or a legal process, a healing framework, that can become your book. If you run a course, the course modules become the chapters and voila, you have a book. If you lead a six-week coaching program, welcome to your six-part book. Podcast host, pick your top ten best episodes and there are your ten chapters.

One of our Thought Leader clients, Simona Spark, felt she could not write her book because English was not her first language. She felt more comfortable speaking so we first worked on her signature talk. She booked stages. She spoke at TEDx. Then, she turned her talk content into a bestselling memoir.

Sometimes clients come to Thought Leader Academy and say, "I have limited time, I don't like to write, but I really want a book." Then I suggest a collaborative book. Choose their theme, write one chapter, and invite ten other fascinating individuals with expertise on the topic to each contribute a chapter. When Megan McCann called me in February one year and said, "I want a book out by a June event I'm hosting and I want it to be a bestseller," I said, "Game on." I recommended the collaborative book, which became *Soul Success*. Megan wrote a chapter, her contributors wrote their chapters in two weeks each, and by June 21, she was holding her bestselling book in time for her big event.

Our Thought Leader client, Pirie Grossman, got hit hard by Covid. A few days into her isolation, she found that reading inspiring stories of people who'd reinvented themselves after adversity lifted her heart and accelerated her healing. She got the idea for a book that would give people the experience she'd just had, but she had low energy from the virus and wanted the book to be done quickly. I suggested the interview book. Pirie had always loved interviewing people, so, from bed, she put out a call for people to share inspiring stories of reinvention.

Tim Ferris wrote a one and a half page introduction to *Tribe of Mentors* and the rest of the book was published interviews he'd conducted over email. That book became a *New York Times* bestseller.

There is always a (easier than you think!) way to do a book.

So, what book category is most aligned for your book?

Choose the one that resonates most and let's move to the next step.

Step Four: The Structure

In the beginning, writing a book was an arduous process that took me years to accomplish. I would see colleagues publishing a book every year and feel physical longing. I wanted to be that prolific, but I kept starting and stopping. Rewriting the first chapter forty-five times (this is not an exaggeration), letting other things like zeroing my inbox and organizing my closets were more important. I kept saying, "I'm such a slooooooow writer," and of course that thought only reinforced itself as the story I was creating in my life.

One week, I felt so fatigued from my resistance and self-doubt and slow ass pace on my own that I decided to procrastinate by reverse engineering one hundred of the top bestselling nonfiction books to see what they all did to create such impact and success. In this case, the procrastination paid off. I journaled and diagramed and distilled the "moves" of these books into three main things present in almost every one of them. What emerged was what I now teach in Thought Leader Academy (and use in all my own thought leader books). My secret Three-Part Bestselling Book Framework.

The framework was a game changer. I went from publishing a book every three to five years to publishing TWO books in one year. I shared it with our clients, and they started completing books in record time. Last year, a few TLAers wrote their books in six weeks. If you're writing a nonfiction (personal growth, self-help or Thought Leader book), this three-part framework will take away the blank page and fast-track every book you write.

The framework is based on three key components that I call:

S-S-S

The first *S* is your STORY.

Each of you has an origin story. Like superheroes. You likely know that Batman witnessed his parent's murder behind the movie theater in Gotham City and grew up to defend the city against crime. You have an origin story of your mission, your work, your book topic. You experienced something, learned something, discovered something, and these experiences called you to the book you are now going to write.

We start books with the origin story so the reader makes a connection with you. They see that you are THE person to take them on this journey, to help them overcome their challenge, or achieve their dream.

Before they jump aboard the raft with you, they'll want to know you've faced what they're facing, that you found higher ground, that you have a skeleton key to get them where they want to go. In the first *S*, you also want to share all the cool s— you've done. If you have a doctorate, share that with your reader. If you've been symptom free from something or created a multi six-figure business or helped one person heal from or transform this thing you teach, let the reader know. If you've brought your work to thousands of people in an online course or spoken at conferences or been featured somewhere inspiring, SHARE it!

One of our TLA clients was a graduate of Yale and had spoken at Stanford, UCLA, and NYU. "I don't want to say any of that in my book," she said. "It's bragging."

I offered to her that the readers don't know us from a nail in the wall yet. If someone is offering to teach me about making more money,

WRITE

but they don't tell me they run an eight-figure business or have helped other people at my business level scale to multiple seven figures, I may not keep reading. I asked her if she would've wanted to work with me as much if she didn't know I'd published books, been featured in *The New York Times* and on *Oprah* and TEDx?

"Definitely not," she said. "I want to do all those things."

It's not bragging to let people know why they can trust us, that this is not our first "rodeo" as they say. Sharing our credentials, lived experience, and results is SERVICE. It's what the reader (and your future client) needs and deserves to know so they are confident continuing the journey with you.

Make a list now of the key "origin" moments of your book topic and mission.

Then list some of the awesome things you've done related to your mission and topic.

You can also do this in the workbook or I'll coach your virtually here:

The second *S* is THE SITUATION.

In the first *S*, you're sharing intimately with the reader about your journey, your background, and experience. You've invited them to take the trip with you and what you envision for them on the other side.

In the second part of your book, write about the situation. This is where you zoom out from the individual to the universal. In his mega-bestseller, *Profit First*, Mike Michalowicz starts with his personal story of being an entrepreneur, making tons of money, but keeping none of it and working so hard and long he never saw his family. Then he zooms out and says, "hey, I'm not just some loser who can't get my act together." Something like 90 percent of entrepreneurs work crazy hours, make gross revenue, but they take none of it home, or worse, are even in debt. In seconds online or using AI, you can find stats, research, and data on your topic. One of our Thought Leaders, Justine Sloane, wrote a book about her time in the fitness industry, the abusive mindset and treatment of women, and how she took all that and created powerful programs for women to build healthy, empowered relationships with their bodies and channel their energy into creating amazing visions and success in their lives. While doing a quick research sprint, she found a study that showed 94 percent of women in America at the time of the study said they "hated their bodies." Hated! She used this statistic to show the reader that the challenge she's going to help them with is epidemic, that it's unacceptable, and that it could change.

In the second *S* of *Profit First*, Mike shows the stats of entrepreneurs. He tells us if we don't take different actions, we'll never break free of the entrepreneur trap, and he paints a painful picture of the costs if we don't change: exhaustion, burn-out, ruined relationships. Mike is not a sadist. He's not using his book to punish the reader. He's doing something really important, which you get to do in the second *S* of your book. He's ripping off the denial blanket and demonstrating that we are not alone, and that if we don't change, we'll be doomed to this path forever. He's creating a buy in for the reader to be willing to CHANGE.

Our brains are wired to resist change. The amygdala in our brain thinks change is dangerous.

Now the second *S* would suck if it was a two-part book structure, but luckily, the best is yet to come.

The third *S* is THE SOLUTION!

Eureka! Our reader knows from reading part two that things will not likely go well for them if they stay on their current trajectory. They are bought in and poised to change. In the third *S*, we give them the solution.

The solution is the remainder of your book. It may be three chapters, ten, twelve. If you have a twelve-week coaching program, you can make chapter one your story. Chapter two is the situation and chapters three to fourteen are the steps in your program. There's so much more I want to show you on structure, but so this book does not become 800 pages long, we're going to move to an exciting technique that will allow the book to almost start "writing itself." You can download the worksheet for this section or go through all the steps with me virtually:

Step Five: The Story Bank

When our clients reach the stage of knowing their idea, category, and structure, a new gremlin sometimes appears: what exactly is going to fill out this structure and generate thousands of words on the page. This is what I call the "what the heck goes in this thing?" gremlin. I started thinking about ways to circumvent this gremlin. When recovering addicts go through a twelve-step program, one of the most formidable steps is step nine: making amends for past harms. So the creators of the twelve steps put in step eight as a preparation step. Instead of jumping right into confronting everyone the addict has harmed, they simply "make a list" of the people. It's a lot less terrifying to make a list of names than to go hunt down your college roommate, look them in the eye, and apologize for eating their food from the fridge and throwing up on their shoes the night you were so drunk you couldn't find the bathroom. Step eight let's people make forward movement, but it chunks the bigger task down a bit. Once the list is made, it can be easier to just take one name at a time, one day at a time, and say "sorry."

Hemingway had the same fear of the blank page that most of us do. While doing my masters at Northwestern, I read that Hemingway always ended his writing sessions in the middle of a sentence. That way he would never have to face the blank page. He'd just have to finish the sentence, and by then, he'd be in motion. He could write the next sentence. And so on. I find it comforting to hear that Hemingway feared writing. Maya Angelou too. In one interview, Maya was reported to say that when she started each book she feared, "this would be the one when they find out I don't know what I'm doing." These writers are considered amongst the greats in the world. True geniuses. And they felt afraid too.

None of us feels like we know what we're doing. So, we get to create a way to trick our minds into taking action even when we're intimidated by the bigger task. We get to do a step eight before we start writing the actual book. My solution: The Story Bank.

Before I ask our clients to start writing their books, I offer them this technique.

Open a new notes file on your phone or fresh page in your journal.

Think about your book/writing topic. Then just start brainstorming once a day for a few minutes of all the stories, moments, and ideas that relate to your topic. For example, key moments when you realize that your seemingly random journey in life was all really pointing to this important work that you're doing in the world. Add rock bottom moments, challenges, breakthroughs, victory moments, mission moments. Add the unique ideas, paradigms, and structures, techniques and strategies that you've developed and innovated.

Then add to this the wonderful stories of your own transformation and those of the people you've helped with your work.

For story bank entries, you're not writing out the whole event or idea. Just a title and a few bullets, whatever brief entry you need to pull the idea back to mind when you're ready to slot it into your book. A tag phrase, a couple of words, or a sentence will be more than enough.

When preparing to write this book, I entered many things in the story bank. One obvious entry was the story of the book that saved my life. In a book about helping others write books and changings lives as a thought leader, that was a key mission moment. It's also part of my origin story of why I do the work I do, why I write books, and founded Thought Leader Academy.

I didn't write all the detail of the Boston airport and the color of the book cover. The story bank entry was: Boston airport, book saved life.

Then I moved on to the next entry.

The Boston airport and finding that book was a big mission moment. It's the foundation of my entire mission. But the story bank is not just for those whole life-changing ideas. Include medium, small, and even "tiny" transformation moments related to your topic as well. In my story bank for this book, I added creating *S-S-S*, the white-water rafting trip with my family that relates to a great book introduction, and even the Mark Twain quote, "The difference between the right word and the almost right word is the difference between lightning and a lightning bug."

Reading an exquisite word that reminds me of the power of the craft didn't change the whole trajectory of the rest of my life and certainly didn't save it. But it's a quote that shoots shivers through my arms that I thought I might want to include, especially paired with the quote from Sean Dougherty, "There is someone out there with a wound in the exact shape of your words." These quotes both speak to the power of writing and the importance of sharing our work with the world, so they went into the story bank.

The beautiful part about the story bank is that there's no pressure; again, we're not asking ourselves to formulate this amazing bestselling book. There's no agenda to figure out where these entries will go; you're just logging ideas at this stage. Suddenly though, I see this every time I teach the Bestselling Book Intensive, like magic, your mind begins to register that you really do have a lot of content, that you do have expertise, that you have ideas, that you have A BOOK.

One final note on the story bank. Something very special happens when we start it. Entries will start revealing themselves to you in unexpected moments. Your content starts pouring to you like an inexhaustible fountain. Ideas start coming while you're making spaghetti or walking your dog or brushing your teeth before you go to bed. And suddenly you're gonna think, oh my gosh, yes, this would be perfect for my book. People will "randomly" send you quotes and links that have the exact thing that will back up a point you're making in that next section. It is like that beautiful W.H. Murray quote, "That the moment one definitely commits oneself, then Providence moves too. All sorts of things occur to help one that would never otherwise have occurred. A whole stream of events issues from the decision, raising in one's favor all manner of unforeseen incidents and meetings and material assistance, which no man could have dreamed would have come his way."

The story bank is the best kind of Pandora's box.

Then, and only when you've worked up some solid entries in that story bank, you can transfer those beautiful gems and nuggets of ideas into your book structure.

Step Six: The Book Map

Most of our clients hate the word "outline." So I created The Book Map. The book map is simply a document where you put together the pieces of your book, in the optimal order. Happily, once you've done the first six steps in this process, the book map (or outline) is quite easy to do. If you're tactile, you can put a big wall-sized, Post-it up in your work space with the letters *S-S-S* across the top. Then start putting your story bank ideas onto colorful sticky notes and begin, like a rainbow-colored jigsaw puzzle, putting the entries in the section where they best fit.

Another of our clients likes neatness and order. She created her book map in a Google spreadsheet. She had a section for each *S* and filled those perfectly uniform cells with entries from her story bank until she had a map of her entire book. You can use rolled up butcher paper to map your book, an accordion notebook, a word document. No way to do it right or wrong. See what visual excites you most and use that one. As you start transferring entries from the story back, you'll start to easily see what parts go where once you have a bird's eye visual. This entry is part of your origin story. This one is definitely in the solution number four chapter. Once you have the map, you can let go of the big picture and focus 100 percent on writing the one next section. The universe is holding the big picture in the form of your glorious map.

Step Seven: Monetizing the Book

Sometimes people come up to me and say, "I want to write a book and then retire to a Caribbean island, living off the royalties." This is a beautiful vision and I will stand for anyone who wants to fulfill it AND because the number of authors who make millions per year on book sales exclusively is a fraction of those who write books and many of them spent many years eating ramen and saving up for a car. (We've all heard the stories of J.K. Rowling scribbling Harry Potter on the pub napkin.) I recommend, you fast-track your abundance by ADDING something to your book. You can add a course, a coaching program, consulting services, a membership, retreats, paid keynotes-anything that lights you up, aligns with your zone of genius, and thrills you will be great. If you already have a program, course, product, or service related to your book topic, hooray! You're ready to supersize your abundance. If you don't have one of these in place, I have great news for you too. You can take your book content and TURN that into a course, retreat, coaching program, service, or other product. WIN-WIN.

I'll share my best overall strategies for monetizing your bigger mission in a coming chapter, but right up front, here is my favorite way to leverage your book as a portal to big abundance.

Two years ago, a colleague said, "I don't even want people to finish reading my book."

You don't! I thought. As a writer, I was horrified.

"I want them to be so inspired about the work I do that they stop reading halfway through and hire me!"

I got it. Any of us with a business, product, or service probably wants the same thing. I love a good quest, so I went out to search for what would make a reader do this. That's when we started creating book portals.

A book portal, or book resource page, is an online place where readers go from the pages of the book, to an interactive experience. When a reader buys a book, there's a one-way nature to the relationship. You don't have a way to send them a text or DM and ask how it's going. Do they have questions? How can I serve? But when they give their name and email to you at a website or online book page, you are now in a relationship. We're now collaborators with our readers. We can mentor, serve, support, assist, and change their lives.

What would make a reader leave the book and interact in this way? Answer: a valuable FREE resource that complements the book and gives them a desired WIN.

To come up with ideas for your resource, start with your own habits as a reader. I started noticing all the times I wished there was more support in the books I read. If the author wrote about a meditation, I longed for a way to download an audio of that mediation with background music so I could truly implement. Sometimes I wished for a worksheet or workbook. Or some behind the scenes of the author's writing journey. I "resource banked" these ideas, and when it came time to publish, *The Science of Getting Rich for Women*, I'd created a workbook, guided exercises, demos, interviews, a whole "world of the book" ready for our readers to explore.

We want to make the resource(s) EASY for the reader to access. We started using QR codes like you see in this book. The reader can hover a phone and instantly be on the page. I've created resources for you throughout this book. I just ask myself as I write, what would create a bigger win for the reader, and then I see if I can make a resource to enhance what I'm teaching.

Look at your favorite nonfiction books and you may see authors generously sharing in this way. You can do a quiz and assessment like Mike in *Profit First*, a downloadable template, a workbook, or worksheet. You can take readers to a page of menus or recipes. One of our clients who loves music made a book playlist, which was very popular with his readers.

The point of this is generosity first. The result is that your ideal people will want to work further with you. Once they download your resource or hang out in your book portal, you can send them a message. You can invite them to a masterclass or workshop or retreat. After reading your book and taking in your awesome content, the people who need you will want more. No matter how incredible your book is, most people need more mentorship, community, and accountability to implement change and transform. By inviting them into a generous relationship with you, you can let them know how they can do that.

I've had the gift of working with clients in Thought Leader Academy who read *The Science of Getting Rich for Women*, went to the portal, used the resources, and emailed to ask to join TLA. As a reader, I went through almost all of Vishen Lakhiani's content on his portal for *The Code of the Extraordinary Mind* and then joined Mind Valley's (his company's) annual membership.

Mike Michalowicz offers people who take his assessment the opportunity to talk with his team, to work with a Profit First accountant or coach. One of my mentors, Fabienne Fredrickson included a business assessment in her book, *The Leveraged Business*. In less than five minutes of their time, the assessment offers personalized results on the stage of their business and a customized strategy to help them get to the next level. It's short, focused, and really valuable. I bet most people who read that book took her up on it.

In fact, I know lots of them did because it's been the main sales strategy and her multi-million dollar-a-year business for the last couple of years.

A fun way to "book portal or resource bank" is to sit with a friend and brainstorm. Talk through where your ideal reader/client gets stuck.

And then create a resource that will powerfully help them overcome that hurdle.

Write your ideas for a book resource or portal now. Or use the workbook or virtual training:

Step Eight: Creating Time to Write

If we are in the room or on Zoom together at the Bestselling Book Intensive, I ask how many people have a time gremlin? Meaning, do you have a fear you don't have the time to write a book?

Life's already busy. There's hardly any time, so when exactly is this writing going to happen? As a mother who runs two businesses and is in a loving marriage, I get it. We don't have the time. It's never going to be convenient to write a book or launch a course or go on a wildly awesome trip.

For most of us, the three week artist's residency in a cabin in the woods or year-long sabbatical is not easily accessible. Here's the good news. We can write it anyway. We can write the book anyway, now. I'm going to show you how you can take some of the pressure out of that balloon around time and the work it will take to do your book.

To tackle the overwhelm of the workload, I use a technique called The Magic Equation. Instead of thinking, *I have to write a whole book!* (this will send our brain into fire alarms and tornado swirls), we can come at the book a different way.

First, estimate the number of pages you imagine your book will be. Look at a few books on your shelf or flip through your digital library.

Books used to run around 350 pages for a novel or memoir and around 250 for other nonfiction. More recently (you might feel some relief to hear), Thought Leader books are coming in around 150 pages. Don't get too caught up in the number, just pick one for the equation.

Next, decide the due date for your book. When would you like to hold that finished manuscript in your hand? Six months? Three? Six weeks? Make a note of your desired finish date.

Now decide how many days a week you can devote to writing. Some of our clients do every day, some do just weekdays, so five, some only weekends, so two.

Then, divide the number of pages by the number of weeks by the number of days, and you'll see how many pages you get to write each day to meet your goal.

Here's an example: say you want to write a two hundred page thought leader book. You want to write four days per week and finish in twelve weeks (three months.) Your number of pages per day is four.

Check in with your body. Does writing four pages feel better than writing "a whole book!?" It does to me. Just like using the story bank and book map, the magic equation can take the spin out of your head a bit and also bring focus to your writing sessions. All you need to do is four pages or two. Or you can write a 365 page novel in one year.

Most of our Thought Leader clients want to write their books fast and choose between six and twelve weeks.

Once we know our page count per session, we get to find the TIME to generate those pages. Using my secret time strategies, I have been able to help every single client I've worked with find the time to do their book. It's always there. Here are my three favorite strategies.

TIME JOURNAL

If you've ever done a money log or a food journal, the time journal is the same idea. For at least a week, you are going to log every single thing you do. This will be stultifying and it'll make you want to just go write already. Just like becoming aware of what we're eating or how much money we're spending, the time journal shows us where the time is going. You're not trying to change or analyze anything, simply block by block, write down what you do and for how long.

7:00-7:15 a.m. shower

7:15-7:30 a.m. meditate

7:30-8:00 a.m. breakfast/ check email

On and on.

The only requirement here is honesty. Because until we see where the time is actually going, we won't be empowered to make the changes. Most of us feel like there's absolutely no time, and yet we may find that in the evenings, we're watching three back-to-back episodes of a Netflix show, for example, or we're spending forty-five minutes on a phone call to a friend or family member who we love but could have a really beautiful fifteen-minute call, which opens up thirty minutes. There are the occasions where one of my clients had multiple jobs and is a single parent. In these occasions, there really isn't much time. In which case we have a decision to make. Get some help, exchange for child care, get up an hour earlier, or stay up an hour later. In order to get the *Science of Getting Rich for Women* book done in six weeks, while running the two companies, being a parent, and all the other things in my life, I chose to get up at five every morning. I promised myself I wouldn't need to do it forever, just until the book was done. I finished on time and I liked the extra hour so much I kept the new schedule.

The time journal is to give us clarity and choice. Once we've logged a week, we can analyze. I don't need to cut out all my Netflix shows, but could I write for an hour and only watch one show? At the end of the year, will I be happiest if I finished the book or watched twenty-five series? No matter how great the shows are (and there are so many great ones!), I'm going to be happiest knowing I wrote the book.

Try jotting down your time for today, just to get started. What do you see in your time log? Are there any swaps you could make to open time to write?

TIME SCHEDULING

An early mentor of mine said, "If it gets scheduled, it gets done." Scheduling our writing time won't guarantee we do it, but it's a powerful start. I encourage my clients to schedule writing time the way they do their most important appointments. How do you ensure you will make the flight or the dentist's appointment or the session with your client? Electronic calendar, phone alarm, reminder emails? Whatever you do for the most important time commitments, do the same for your writing. This sends your subconscious a message that you're serious, that the writing is important, that you intend to bring this book to fruition.

A number of years ago, I had a session with a new coach. She asked me my top three goals for the year and then said, "Great, open up your calendar." I felt like someone asked me to take off my clothes. "I want to see how serious you are about your goals," she said. "When I look at your calendar, I should see your time devoted to your highest priorities, which you say is becoming a published author." I didn't have a single writing session scheduled. Not a one. From that day forward, the writing time was there.

Take a few minutes and open next week's calendar. Find at least one day you could write and block out that time. Maybe choose a happy color. Follow through. Do it.

What gets scheduled gets done.

Virginia Wolfe said that in order to write, a woman needed "a room of one's own." Sometimes through, we don't have a room, or even a whole hour. What do we do then? Enter strategy three.

THE TIME WEDGE

It took seven years for me to become a mother so when my son was born, I was understandably ecstatic. I also got my first book deal, the other big dream of my life. It was wildly exciting. AND, I didn't know how I was going to get the book done! There was no sleep. No free time.

I had a newborn. I hardly showered. I began to sweat when I thought about that deadline approaching, until I met Rebecca.

One night, I went to a two-hour workshop at a local writing school in Chicago. It was my first outing without my son strapped to my body in the sling.

Rebecca shared with the writers how she had four children under the age of five. No nanny, no babysitter, and how she refused to give up on her dream of writing a book. In fact, she'd gotten a book deal for a trilogy, and like me, she knew that she would never be okay with herself if she let that dream go.

"I wrote all three books-on time-never having more than thirty minutes at a time to write," she said.

Four children! Under five! Three books! I was stunned. Meeting her annihilated every excuse I had.

THE WRITING WEDGE

From the day I met Rebecca forward, I opened myself to a new writer's life. One formed wedge by wedge. I call a writing wedge any increment of time under forty minutes. As I started reclaiming writing time from the "throwaway" minutes I'd spent scrolling social media, shopping for groceries vs having them delivered, checking my email multiple times an hour, etc., my book started to form. Twenty, fifty, one hundred pages forged, never having more than an hour at a time.

Since that day, I've written in dentist office waiting rooms, the school pick-up line, in the time it takes between a nice juicy piece of sea bass marinating in my fridge to get to the grill. I've written at airport gates, even pulled over in a parking lot at the grocery store. I wrote *Ghost House* entirely in thirty-minute wedges. The writing wedge has worked for clients too. A teacher took her forty-five minute free period, skipped the chitchat in the teacher's lounge, and wrote in her car every day, five days a week, until the book was done. The writing wedge allows us to write a book regardless of our other commitments. If you, like me, have a full, hugely committed life, it will save your ass.

To make the most of my wedges, I spend a few minutes in the shower every morning deciding exactly what I will tackle in my wedge that day. We don't want to spend fifteen of our thirty minutes wondering where to begin or what to write. I look at my book map the night before, pull some ideas from the story bank, and in the shower, like Heminway ending his previous day's work midsentence, I begin the wedge in my mind. When the time comes, I have momentum, I have energy flowing. As Steven Pressfield says, "I've evoked the Muse."

Invitation: look at your schedule between now and when you go to bed tonight. Find one fifteen-minute window and claim it for your book. Use that time to story bank or book map if you haven't done those yet. Or get that next sentence, paragraph, or even page DONE! I'm excited for you to try the wedge! You've got this!

Step Nine: Accountability

When I was a kid, I was on the swim team. In high school, our 200-meter relay team made it to regionals. I was the anchor. The success of those other three amazing swimmers and my team at large rested on me. My coach timed our "splits" (personal time for our leg of the relay), and she came to me perplexed. You never hit that time when you swim the individual event. Same two lengths of the pool, same flip turn, same body, and yet I could never go as fast when I was only racing for myself. But no way in hell I was letting my team members, heaving up water on the deck while I finished that race, down.

The difference, I could tell my coach now, was accountability. Remember my story of freezing after I met the literary agent? How I spent three weeks unable to write a word? The breakthrough out of that insanity was accountability. Hiring that writing coach to whom I'd invested and was expecting that next chapter ensured that I got it done. Like working with a personal trainer for workouts, we will always do more when someone else knows and is counting on us. You likely know by now what methods of accountability work for you.

- A buddy
- A class
- A coach
- A mentor
- A tracking app or device
- A community

I heard that when Jerry Seinfeld wanted to try new material but felt fear about getting up on stand-up stages, he hung up a wall calendar and marked an *X* on every day he did stand-up. He said he wanted to see that calendar full of *X*s at the end of the month. The ritual of marking the days kept him accountable. He didn't want to see any open squares. After hearing Jerry's story, I bought myself a little paper calendar from Paper Source, carried it around with me, and made a *W* every time I did a wedge. It became a bit of an obsession, seeing a whole row, then a whole month of *W*s.

In my journey to empowered thought leader, I have used, and still use, every one of the accountability structures listed above. In Thought Leader Academy, we built multi-levels of accountability right into our curriculum: accountability partners, success pods of six to eight that meet monthly, implementation "write in" sessions, Zoom writing parties, trackers, workshops, masterclasses, and in-person retreats. No writer or book left behind!

Employing accountability doesn't make us weak; it means we're smart. You want to fast-track your financial income, book publication date, getting on the TEDx stage? Put yourself in a position to be accountable. Ensure whoever or whatever you choose loves you, sees the higher vision for you, and won't let you walk back from your goals. For whatever reason, we just won't show up for ourselves the way we will when someone else is waiting for our results. It may be part saving face, part image management, part the energy and motivation that someone cheering us on and holding the vision of our higher potential gives us. I'm at the point I don't care why accountability works. I just know that it does, and you'll do in three months what you could do in a year (or ten!) when you have it.

So: what accountability are you going to put in place to write your book?

And just in case there are any remaining dragons at the gate between you and going all the way with your book or writing, call up a book or author who has made a powerful impact on you.

Got one?

Let's together offer gratitude to that author. Imagine her walking through the fears, the time constraints, the gremlins. Imagine Brené Brown being told a book about shame was stupid and no one would read it and how she then printed the book herself and sold it out of the back of her car. Imagine Jack London receiving five hundred rejections before anyone would publish his work. Imagine Tony Morrison refusing to bend when publishers resisted her, breaking "the white gaze." Imagine the book that changed your life, that gave you hope, that opened up a new perspective for you.

Imagine what would have not happened for you if she'd talked herself out of it, been seduced by the voices of others, or her inner critic.

Imagine what wouldn't have happened for the world if Don Miguel Ruiz didn't give us *The Four Agreements* or Eckhart Tolle, *A New Earth*? In one of his incredible poems, David Whyte writes, "People are starving. And one good word is food for thousands."

People are starving and you have the food. You have the gift and you will attract all the time, money, and everything you need for the journey.

Spend just a few seconds imaging that author you chose, who wrote a book that changed your life, is now handing their torch to you. No matter what the gremlins say, YOU are now someone's Brené Brown, Amy Tan, Elizabeth Gilbert, Gabby Bernstein. Let's Go!

CHAPTER SIX

Speak

The incredible thing about writing a book is that you become an instant expert on your topic. You have major credibility now. Particularly as a bestselling author. So far, every one of our Thought Leader Academy clients who've implemented our step-by-step roadmap has not only published their books but has hit the bestseller list. I'm obsessed that you get on that list too. Because you're on that list once, and then have the credential of [insert your name] bestselling author, for the rest of your life.

It's a very exciting thing.

AND the challenge, if we only have a book, is that even though we have mucho more credibility as bestselling authors than we did before, the book does not automatically mean the floodgates of impact and income automatically open. To get to our full throttle, we must employ the other four strategies of the Thought Leader Pathway. The book is the foundation. The book starts to open doors. And one of those doors is SPEAKING. In this section, I'm going to show you how powerful it is to add speaking to your thought leader portfolio, how to decide where you might like to speak, what kind of speaking you'd like to do, how to be seen as an irresistible expert, and how to be paid to speak.

Isabella Baumfree was called to be a thought leader. Only no one used that term in the 1800s when she lived. She was enslaved four times before escaping with her infant daughter and later recovering her son in 1828. In 1843, she heard God calling her to speak, to give people who would hear her hope, and to further equal rights for women and all people of color. She was called to lead a movement, and lead she did. She changed her name to Sojourner Truth, and in the face of haters, of mobs, of bigots, she spoke her undeniable message and changed not only history, but she illuminated the hearts and minds of women and men for centuries.

Sojourner Truth had every reason to keep her light hidden, to live below the radar. The dangers she faced were immense. Her very life was on the line. But she spoke anyway because she felt compelled to do so. To do anything less would be to continue the cycle of gross disparity and inequality in the world. Even without learning how to read and write, she authored a book by dictating the words, and her book was so successful she lived off the sales for the rest of her life.

Over a century later, pioneering what would become the coaching industry, Tony Robbins answered the call to speak and write. Speaking has been at the core of Tony's mission for decades, and as a result, he has empowered over fifty million people from one hundred countries around the world through his audio programs, educational videos, and live speaking events. You may be a Tony Robbins fan, or not, but regardless, he is undeniably one of the most impactful speakers on the planet. Tony's speaking events fill hundred-thousand person sports stadiums, but you don't have to speak to a hundred thousand people at a time to make an impact.

The year I started Thought Leader Academy, a friend of mine named Mary passed away from cancer. She was a beloved friend to many women I knew in Chicago. One of the women had the idea to gather at her home and listen to recordings of some of the talks Mary gave. Mary had been sober for over twenty-five years, she'd gone to divinity school, had become a spiritual counselor, and she'd often been asked to speak at local community groups. We sat on overstuffed chairs in the living room, closed our eyes, and listened as Mary's voice filled the room to the ceiling. I cried through most of the morning, but what struck me sitting there, as we heard Mary's laughter and wisdom and the deep, profound joy she took in connecting with other humans, was how alive she still was. She was palpably back in the room with us, even though she was no longer living bodily. I was struck that day with the smell of lemon zest and chamomile tea hanging in the room, how many people will never get this gift. Never experience the person they love being in the room with them because that person never got up in front of a room or a camera, hit record, and shared their spark. It matters that we share the music inside us while we're here. Mary's recorded talks proved to me that day the power of legacy. Just like writing a book, your ideas and heart and love through speaking will live long beyond when we're on this planet.

I'm guessing you can think of a talk or podcast or sermon you've heard that rocked your world. Martin Luther King Jr.'s, "I Have a Dream," Amanda Gorman's speech at President Biden's inauguration, and if you haven't heard J.K. Rowling's Harvard commencement address on failure, run to YouTube this moment and watch it. What's the talk that's made the biggest impact on you?

Clients come to Thought Leader Academy with the same calling as Sojourner Truth and Tony Robbins. They say, "I feel I need to be on bigger stages." That call is not random. I believe the call is Resonance at work. Further, I believe your call to write and speak is being sourced by the people you are here to serve, like a universe level call and response.

And even though you are worthy, capable, and meant for this, just like with writing a book, almost on cue, the moment we say, "Yes! Let's go speak," enter the gremlins.

Who do you think you are?
No one wants to hear you.
You're not a celebrity.
You don't have a big enough following.

What would make someone pick YOU as the keynote speaker?

My clients feel the same tension I felt, the rub between being called to share the treasures inside, alongside the dislike of having the (in this case literal), spotlight on ourselves. We feel the calling to speak and some part of us knows the pull is true. It's our soul. The real deal. But other parts start chiming in. *Oh, come on. You're no Brené Brown.*

Then they actually book a talk, using the strategies I'll share here, and even more gremlins arrive. I actually have to get up on that stage! What am I going to say? What am I going to teach? Can I make money doing this? How much should I charge? And we're back in the swirl.

Just like with book writing, there are so many obstacles to speaking that many people give up before they start. It all just feels too daunting. Too much. Every one of these pieces in and of itself is like a big wall that we have to scale. But it doesn't have to be hard. You're a thought leader now. You've got me. I've given over one thousand talks and presentations: masterminds, masterclasses, workshops, keynotes, lunch and learns, guest speaking, panel discussions, podcasts and more podcasts, virtual events, in-person events, to four people in a musty writing studio to a hotel ballroom of one thousand people bursting at the seams. I've helped all our clients who want to speak, do so. There's no wall we can't scale together. Starting today. Those walls are coming down.

Because if you're reading this book and feel excited to speak on any of those types of stages and platforms, it's because you're meant to do it. You wouldn't have the calling or the vision if you weren't. So let's go ahead and just remove these problems one by one, these challenges one by one, and get you out sharing your message.

Now. As Mary so clearly demonstrated, time is essential. There's urgency to you getting out there now. If Mary had waived off the invitations to speak until she was wiser, more polished, more evolved, more something, we wouldn't still have her here with us, anytime, at the push of a button. Mary wasn't speaking in some twenty thousand person football stadium. She was sharing a room full of twenty people in a library basement in her home town. But not now, now she can be heard all over the world-all over the universe.

Step One: Your Speaking Vision

Where would you like to speak? On Zoom with the host of your favorite entrepreneur podcast? On the TEDx stage? In front of a standing room only crowd at Tony Robbins' next event? Step one is to define where you want to speak and add to this list until you have one hundred ideal speaking venues. Yep, one hundred.

The One Hundred

When I was first aspiring (more accurately struggling) to write and get published, I would send out an essay or story or book pitch, and if it was rejected, I would interpret that rejection as that the piece was no good and shove it into a dungeon-like folder on my computer. If I received a personal rejection letter with a critique of why the piece was rejected, I would feel so much shame that I wouldn't write sometimes for weeks, honestly, sometimes for months. I stayed in this cycle for several years, and I'm sure it will not shock you to learn that the number of published pieces = zero. I felt demoralized until I read about a woman on the website, Lit-Hub.

The woman described feeling exactly like I did. Except she'd been submitting pieces a lot longer than I had. After years of rejection and nothing to show for it, she decided to quit. But before she shut down her laptop for good, she decided to do a kind of swan song. She made a mission to get one hundred rejections in one year.

WOW! I was awed. I understood though, that this act of seeking the one hundred rejections gave her the power back. She couldn't feel upset because she'd sought the rejections. She flipped the script. She changed her STORY. She made rejection the win. The thing that I'm sure the wise part of her understood from the start was that in order to get one hundred rejections, you have to submit at least one hundred pieces of writing, or the same piece of writing to one hundred different places. What do you think happened?

By the end of the year, she'd been published three times, won an award, and been granted a fully paid writing residency. (Essentially camp for writers where you go off in nature, have all your meals taken care of for you, write all day, and hang out with other artists in the residency in the evenings, aka: heaven.) By going ALL IN for the one hundred, she'd created her most successful writing year ever. She didn't quit (who would after that?), and she gave me and likely hundreds of other writers a big gift and a kick in the ass. Now I'm about a ten out of ten on the sensitivity scale (any other empaths out there?), so I wasn't up for seeking out one hundred rejections. But I was on fire about what I would come to call in Thought Leader Academy, the Power 100. That year I committed to one hundred writing submissions. I got published. I tested the strategy on myself again and again. Every piece of writing I did a Power 100 for has been published. Every one.

In Thought Leader Academy, we use the Power 100 for all kinds of things: book submissions, influencers to promote books, book reviews, guests to appear on our summits, shows and events, strategic partners (more on these in the next chapter), AND we use the Power 100 for speaking!

Speaking involves pitching and in many ways, it's a numbers game. You want to reach out to enough places to get the YESs you desire. Not everyone will book you at first try, so we want to go out strong and get in the habit of regular speaking outreach. If you want to speak one time per month, you may need to reach out to five places to get one booking. We want a robust list so you can focus on action and not get too fixed on any specific response. If you have the calling to speak, you're going to speak.

Think about where you want to speak and think deeply about where your ideal person (the person you want to transform with your words), hangs out and consumes content. Where do they go with their dreams, desires, and questions? Who do they follow online? What events do they attend? Where do they travel and when?

If you're not sure where your ideal person consumes content, talk to some people. Find friends or colleagues or ask around until you find the C-suite women over forty or the moms who homeschool or the six-figure entrepreneurs who are burnt out and ask if they'd take two minutes and tell you their favorite people, places, speakers, events. You can conduct an IG or Facebook poll and ask: best event you attended in the last year, best book, favorite podcast.

My secret shortcut is to visit the events page or social media feed of the top leaders in your industry or niche. Find out where they are speaking and appearing. Even though you may build to those exact stages or podcasts, you'll have a sense of the scope and where your people listen to speakers. You can then go to those podcasts and scroll down to the "you may also like" section. This area may list slightly more approachable podcasts and you can work your way up. Same with conferences. You may not be the keynote, but you could pitch to teach a breakout session or workshop where your shero is headlining. I've spoken at conferences with Marianne Williamson, Clarissa Pinkola Estés (*Women Who Run with the Wolves*), on the same podcasts where Gabby Bernstein and Mel Robbins were interviewed. I've presented at the same conferences as Ann Patchett and Jennifer Eagan and the same stages where David Sedaris and Michelle Obama have presented. I wasn't presenting with them, but at first, we work our way up. Stick with it and these bookings will happen.

"But Sara," my clients say to me, "how will any of these places choose ME to be a presenter or guest?" I teach our Thought Leader Academy clients a process to position themselves as an "irresistible expert" even if they're not professional speakers yet, even if their book isn't out yet. I'm going to give you the three things you'll want to include in your outreach (aka pitch) here. If you want my six-step pitch template that has booked our community over two thousand speaking engagements, where you can fill in a winning pitch like mad libs, click here:

Before I give you the three essential components, there is a prestep. Skip this at your peril! Your first crucial step is to ENROLL YOURSELF. Before you reach out to your ideal speaking events and shows, you want to remind yourself how incredible you are. At our Thought Leader Academy retreats, we sometimes play a game called Hi, I'm Awesome. Participants walk around the room and introduce themselves to each other with their first name and a reason why they are amazing. When I introduce this game, everyone groans. They think it will be embarrassing, awkward. Sometimes it is, for about ten seconds. Then, you should feel the energy in the room. The vibration lifts like a ship on a wave. Think back to your origin story, to the personal growth work you've done. Think back to people you've helped and your unique way of viewing the world, of solving challenges. Since we're not in the room playing Hi! I'm Awesome, write your list.

Right now.

Write ten wonderful, awesome, and amazing things about yourself. Try to make at least half of these relate to the topic(s) on which you want to speak. Not sure what you want to speak on? Go to your book map! You could probably do ten unique talks just using the content from your book. Or create one radical, standing ovation talk based on your bestselling book idea. Your thought leader assets all work together. You can turn talk into book or book into talk, over and over and over.

The 3 Things

If you include these three things in your speaking outreach, you will set yourself apart from 98 percent of people who pitch themselves to speak. Your email or application will sparkle. You will rise to the top of the pile.

Make the pitch a love letter. Make it about THEM.

Most people who want to speak understandably start with themselves. Who they are, what they do: me, me, me. You want to breakthrough the static; start by acknowledging the person or organization you are pitching. Give them an authentic, heartfelt THANK YOU for the work they do in the world, for their contribution to the industry. If you've been to their event or listened to their podcast or watched their show, mention something detailed and specific you loved or that inspired you. No grabbing some generic statement off their website. I'm talking, "In podcast 403, when you talked about color blind casting in period musicals and films, I was so inspired." The more specific the better. I once had a producer book me for a conference because she said, "You were the only person who really read our blog and commented on it. You made it personal. We feel like you care." I did care and I was honored AF to partner with them.

Create a mission bridge.

Once you've recognized their great work and thanked them for it, we want to put ourselves on equal footing. The person you're pitching may have ten million Instagram followers and be far more well-known than you are right now, but in this section, we demonstrate that we're all playing for the same team. Building on the previous example, a speaker could say, "Diversity in the arts is at the core of everything I do. In fact, it's the reason I wrote my upcoming book ____ and why I speak to schools, corporations, and community groups about diversity in teaching staff and the C-suite." When we're working on the same mission, numbers of followers fades to the background. You're two leaders who have an opportunity to collaborate and further the greater shared mission in the world.

Demonstrate value.

Most speaking pitches stick with, "I'd love to talk about women's empowerment. Or conscious parenting. Call me!"

These topics are terrific, but they don't give the podcast producer or speaking booker a tangible sense of what their audience will learn, and why it matters. I recommend our thought leaders list the key audience takeaways and what I call the "benefit of the benefit."

In my interview/presentation/keynote . . .

A quick note here: at the beginning, when I felt as if I was hacking my way through the speaking landscape with a machete, the idea of even sending a pitch to anyone made my forearms sweat. The anticipation of rejection, like it had been with my writing, was acute. So, if any or all of this is making your head swim, you're not alone and I've got you. Grab the template here and you can even watch me train this in our $1 Million Talk masterclass on video so you feel coached as you go:

If this is all new territory for you, start by asking one person you know who already likes you and hosts a podcast if they'd have you on as a guest.

Let's go deeper into your speaking vision and how to get booked on those stages and shows.

As with your book, we'll want to identify our ideal speaking outcomes. Circle any/all of these that are on your speaking vision:

- Inspiring/educating audiences
- Getting paid to speak
- Attracting new leads for your business
- Attracting ideal clients/clients signing up to work with you from the stage
- Speaking as entry point to consulting or coaching in companies

- Product bundles (speaking + volume book sales or speaking + coaching)
- Developing relationships and partnerships with industry leaders
- Other?

Do you want to show up at a conference and be handed a $20,000 check for a keynote? Or do you want to fly out to international destinations and present workshops on the beach? Do you want to share your product or service from the stage and have people lining up in the back to sign up with you? Do you want to host online webinars that leads thousands of people a week to your course? Do you want to speak at Mind Valley or the Omega Institute, The National Poetry Foundation, or Shakespeare and Company bookstore in Paris?

If your calendar was magically populated with your dream speaking engagements, what would you see? Where would you be speaking over the next month, six months? Year?

Now that you've established a speaking vision, you know about the Power 100, you know how to reach out to individuals and organizations to speak, you need one more foundational piece to go out and blow the roof off those venues!

If you're like our current thought leaders, you'll be brave and start pitching organizations, and then one of them will email you one day, "Yes! We'd love to have you." At this point, panic sets in. Ah! I'm going on a stage! WHAT AM I GOING TO SAY?!!

There is so much delicious nuance and strategy to creating a powerhouse, high-converting talk, so I want to give you something to bring relief. Just like the *S-S-S* book framework, I needed something both simple and powerful.

I went back through the hundreds of talks I'd given over the past years. I watched great talks on YouTube. What emerged like a polaroid photo was the Thought Leader Academy framework I call:

THOUGHT LEADER ACADEMY

STAYS

Five letters. Five moves. Five steps to create a high converting, compelling talk that can work for anything from a twelve-minute TEDx style talk to a full-day workshop. Here's the streamlined take on STAYS. If you want more nuance and craft, I'll give you access to my master training here:

S

The first *S* stands for story. We talked about the power of story in the beginning of this book. Neuroscientist Lisa Kron demonstrates in her work that the human brain is wired for Story. Story is how we learn, heal, and change. Neurologically and biologically. Story drops us from our skeptical heads to our receptive hearts. Story allows us to connect to people at the level of their soul. By starting your talks with a story, you'll create deep connection, relatability, that "know, like, and trust" factor psychologists tell us is imperative to so that real rapport will develop. By beginning with story, the audience will feel your heart and believe you are there to serve them.

Choose an opening story that sets up the theme and content of your talk. Use specific sensory details. Put the audience on the top of the mountain or the hospital room or the dorm; put them into your setting. Your story can be personal, gleaned from your life. Or it can be the story of a client you've worked with, something that happened in history, or a story happening today in modern culture. The point is to introduce the theme of your talk in a heart-opening way, in a compelling way, in a way that leaves them excited about where you will take them next.

T

In this part of your talk, you will teach something experiential, a technique, a strategy, a practice that will give your audience a win. Teaching during your talk is generous. Most people love to learn. By teaching during your talk, you'll release any fear about the talk not being valuable. To your ideal person, who is seeking your solution and expertise, the talk will instantly be valuable because they've learned something. Your talk also becomes transformational because your audience is different at the end of your talk than they were at the beginning. You've enriched them. On a subconscious level, you've also demonstrated your authority on your topic, which builds on the trust you created in the opening story.

A

A is for action. To increase the transformational nature of your talk, you invite your audience to talk action. The action can be to download a bonus resource that will support them in implementing what you taught them in the previous section. One of our Thought Leader Academy clients, Katherine Eitel Belt, gives talks multiple times a month. She teaches people how to have what she's coined Courageous Conversations. The action Katherine could give her audience is to use the framework of the Courageous Conversation with at least one person by the time they go to bed that night. Another of our Thought Leader clients teaches nutrition and conscious eating. In the *T* section of her talk, she gives each person in the audience a raisin and guides them through an intuitive eating experience where they take a full two minutes to smell, taste, chew, and eat the raisin. The exercise illuminates the lack of time and consciousness. In the *A* section of her talk, she challenges the audience to eat their next meal with a phone time of a minimum of twenty minutes. The action can be to see in the back of the room if they have questions, or to schedule a time on your calendar to follow up and do a one-to-one strategy session.

Y

The *Y* in STAYS stands for YES. After sharing intimately in your opening story, teaching valuable content that will improve their lives, getting them into participation and transformation by moving them to action, you invite them to integrate what they've learned by YES-ing themselves and YES-ing what they liked most in your talk.

If you're in a live room or on Zoom, you can say, "Let's take a minute to identify what the most important thing is that you're taking away from our time together." Ask them to type this into the chat if you're in a virtual room. In person, you can have people raise their hands and share. By YES-ing the talk, they recognize the value they've received, and most importantly, they've acknowledged what resonated most for them, and thus, take the experience in at a deeper level. They'll be more committed to implement what they've learned and make real change in their lives. *Y-E-S*.

S

The final *S* is for Story. We start with story, we end with story. Studies reveal that audiences, students, and clients remember content told through story 80 percent more and years longer than content presented as data and straight information.

Just like in the opening, your closing story brings the audience back into their hearts. Your closing story can also come from your lived experience. If you talked about being challenged with a health crisis and going to doctor after doctor after doctor and not knowing how to get help or how to solve this crisis that you were in and you teach them some of the techniques you used to come off medication and live symptom-free, your final story can be what your life is like today. This is a "before and after" approach. Your closing story can be an "after" story of a client you've helped. It can be the story of a societal or cultural change related to what you teach. The goal here is to leave the audience on a note of inspiration, possibility, and commitment to change. Whatever story, anecdote, or way you want to do that is perfect. Trust your gut. Use your book story bank for ideas. The perfect way to end your talk is already inside you!

I've used STAYS to create hundreds of talks. I've taught STAYS to thousands of clients and students. Because of STAYS, I can create a talk in minutes. Our Thought Leader clients feel confident pitching because they know that at any length, venue, or audience size, they can easily create and deliver a high value, high-converting talk. Empowered with this framework, you can start pitching and delivering your talks now! Game on!

Finally, once you know how to put a high value, high-converting talk together, you may wonder about pricing, and how to get paid to speak. A few years ago, I realized I'd made over $1 million speaking! I reverse engineered all the ways I'd received money speaking and turned that into a class for our Thought Leader Academy clients called Your $1 Millon Talk. I mentioned several ways when I asked about your ideal speaking outcomes and peer vision. To review, here are the ways I have and now our clients get paid to speak:

- Paid speaker fee
- Sell service or product directly from stage
- Sell service or product in follow-up from speaking
- Sell bundled products (books, course, etc.) or services (coaching, consulting) through speaking
- Sell an affiliate product or service (someone else's program or product on which you receive commissions)
- Speaking sponsors

Clients often ask how much they can expect to be paid for speaker fees. Rates range hugely from organization to organization and can grow exponentially as your experience increases, but here are the rates I see as of the writing of this book:

- Universities/libraries/community groups: several hundred to $1,500
- Larger nonprofits, larger university: talks can go up to $3,000-$10,000
- Corporate keynotes: can be $10,000-$50,000+

You'll want to keep coming back to your vision and desired outcomes when deciding what speaking to pursue. Those big keynote numbers can be alluring, but if you coach stay-at-home moms or entrepreneurs or people not in the corporate events, they may not be the ideal engagements for you. To be selected for corporate keynotes, you'll need a speaker one page reel and to ensure that your topics and expertise match what the companies are focused on and seeking for their employees.

Pricing and speaker assets are such a juicy topic, I could do a whole separate book on it, but I don't want you to have to wait, so I'm going to give you access to the full $1M Talk training, with more details on the ways to generate income through talks, attract sponsors, and the assets you'll need to book them; click here:

While I do give some keynotes, I generated most of the now multi-million dollars I've made speaking through giving free talks at organizations I love where my ideal person hangs out. Once I had a talk at a local writing school. The talk was on mindset for writers. (Basically how to overcome gremlins and get words on the page and books finished.) A tornado hit Chicago, and understandably, almost no one came to the talk. Four brave souls arrived, wet and panting from the wind. I felt the stab of disappointment, then quickly redirected myself. These amazing individuals braved a tornado! They really want to write. I vowed to give them the best workshop of my life. Afterwards, two of them followed me to the parking lot. "Do you coaching privately?" they asked. Both became long-term clients. In addition to the privilege of working with them on several books over five years, between them, they invested over $100K with me and referred friends.

You don't need to speak to stadiums of people to change lives. You can make massive impact and income speaking to intimate groups. I love big stages, those huge screens, the "Madonna" Lavalier mic, and pacing back and forth on a giant platform. AND some of my highest converting events have been to masterminds of twenty on Zoom while wearing sneakers.

In all the speaking I've done, very few venues invite me to "sell" from the stage, meaning many venues will not permit you to make a direct invitation to your program or product while speaking. This is not a problem! What you'll want in these cases is to offer an irresistible free gift, something the audience needs and desires. Just like the free resource you'll embed in your book, you'll offer one at your speaking events too.

Speakers used to say, "Join my mailing list" and pass around a clipboard. Think about yourself as an audience member. None of us wants to join a mailing list. However, if I'm giving a talk on how to book speaking engagements and I share a story about the pitch template I created for my clients and how the first person to try it booked three ideal podcasts in twenty-four hours and it has since booked our clients over two thousand talks and podcasts, people will race to their phones to access the link.

I have offered this free gift while speaking and about 90 percent of the room signs up.

You'll use the same process we used to ideate options for your book resource for your speaking free gift here. You may find you can use the same one you offer in your book. #Multi-purpose win! Think of where your ideal person gets stuck, a challenge they have, or a goal they want to fulfill, and solve just one piece of it for them in the form of a free resource. You can flash a QR code on the speaker or Zoom screen if you're presenting with visuals. You can also set up automated delivery through text message. I used to have the audience text, "BOOK" to the number of the automated service, and after entering their name and email, they'd receive the "Three-Part Bestselling Book Framework."

There are myriad ways to set up your free gift from the stage. The only essential is that the audience must give their name and email in exchange for your resource. That's the way you can follow up with them. Invite them to further trainings, offer to connect by Zoom or phone, invite them to coach with you.

Speaking coach Pete Vargus makes millions each year speaking. In fact, he recently shared during a presentation that he broke the $10M mark through speaking in one year. I saw Pete speak five years ago. He shared the story of being estranged from his father and how one night, he heard a speaker share his take on forgiveness. That one moment made Pete stand up, walk out of the presentation, and call his dad. They reconciled and Pete found his mission: to change lives from the stage. That year Pete gave that talk on stages around the US. He went all in on his $1M Talk. Since then he's spoken thousands of times, trained thousands in conference ballrooms and online, and then attracted a strategic partner and (if I understand things correctly), an investor in his business. When you say yes to write and to speak, doors open.

You have a Million Dollar Talk in you. Or maybe, like Pete, a $10 million talk. Put these strategies into play and make millions while you transform lives.

* * *

Before we move on to strategy three in the Thought Leader Pathway, let's do a neuro-linguistic programming technique called Future Pace.

Imagine it's a few months from now. You've integrated and implemented everything in this chapter. You've created and pursued your ideal speaking vision. You've identified ideal places to speak, sent these organizations and individuals mission-centered, compelling pitches and your calendar is now filled with podcast interviews and bookings for the exact talks you wanted to give.

How does that feel?

You're changing lives and you're experiencing the manifestation of those desired outcomes for impact, inspiration, education, revenue generation, and success.

Stop reading for one to two minutes and envision this as your reality.

How does it feel? What's different or better in your life? Now that you've become an empowered speaker with your thought leadership, notice who you're hanging out with, what new things have come into your life?

What's better, new, and different for your audience members?

For the world?

At any of the images to your thought leader vision board, look at them every day. Remind yourself that what you're seeking is seeking you. And all those people and podcast producers and conference hosts who are planning their content for the next year are saying, "You know what we really need?" and they're describing YOU!

See yourself creating win-win-win-win-win-win. See yourself magnetized for all this good and success NOW.

CHAPTER SEVEN

Build

In his ass-kicking book, *The 10x Rule,* Grant Cardone states that entrepreneurs ever only have one real problem: lack of visibility. Simply put, not enough people know about you and your marvelous work. Is that true for you? If you had 2x or 3x or 10x the visibility in your industry, would your business change? Your income? Impact? For most of us, the answer is YES. Of all the challenges emerging thought leaders face, lack of visibility (translating into lack of potential leads, audience members, students, and new clients), is amongst the very top source of pain. In the third strategy of Thought Leader Academy, Build, we address this issue head on.

As we've discussed, writing your book and speaking to audiences creates massive credibility and a start to industry leadership, but unless the speaking audiences are large, we still need more visibility. As a thought leader, it is your responsibility to find, inspire, and lead a community or audience of those you are here to serve.

The biggest question our clients have is HOW? How exactly are we to accomplish this task? Then, once we find the HOW (I will share my favorites in this chapter), a deeper fear may emerge. Despite consciously wanting to be known, to serve, to contribute, we are subconsciously absolutely terrified of becoming more visible. Many of us experience this odd paradox, also known as "chaotic vibration," where a part of us wants to shine our light on that stage and another part is damn scared of the potential judgment, criticism, rejection that could come with increased eyes on us and our work. You're not crazy if you feel this way. We see celebrities and influencers facing all kinds of pushback. We hear "haters gonna hate" and trolls sending Brené Brown messages like "less research, more Botox" messages. If we don't bring up and release our fears, we'll find all manner of excuses to keep us from being more visible. We'll send ourselves running right back under our duvet covers. We'll revert to being consumers rather than creators.

I remember in a training years ago, the facilitator said, "If you had to double your audience in one week, in order to get a kidney transplant for your child, what would you do to ensure that result?" We called out ideas: hand out flyers at the hospital of parents who are going through the same thing, start an online movement using a digital petition, take out time on a TV network and share the invitation, wear a giant sandwich board bearing my company name and website at a busy intersection, go door-to-door or DM people on Instagram, offering a way to opt into my audience. The facilitator asked how many people were taking that level of action. Not one of us raised our hand.

I prefer a more cheerful scenario. Imagine if someone said they'd give you a million dollars by the end of the week if you doubled your audience. If you're like me, you'd drop anything else you'd scheduled and spend every minute reaching out to people, networking, pitching, and go ALL IN to have people join your Facebook page.

Sometimes, I've truly not known what to do to build an audience, but often we have all kinds of creative ideas. And the fear of judgment is not the only obstacle. Another root is the fear that no one will "pick up what we're putting out." We'll throw a party and no one will come.

We'll shine that light out hundreds of feet into the water and the whole thing will land like the tree falling silently in the forest. We may fear no response as much, or more, than negative comments.

We often have other fears too. Here are the rest of the "greatest hits":

- I don't have a big advertising budget.
- There are already so many people who do what I do.
- There's so much noise in the marketplace.
- I don't have time to build my visibility.
- I'm afraid I'll take action and it won't work for me.
- Underneath these are more fears:
- Other people are more worthy.
- I don't have something unique or valuable enough to offer or share.
- Other people are more effective, influential, talented, smart, have credentials, rich.

Now we get down to fears about identity.

Fears about safety.

Our subconscious scrolls back through all the leaders who have been targeted, knocked off pedestals, even in some cases, to censorship, or burned at the stake. This sounds dramatic, but your brain feels worried.

Despite our freedom of speech, we believe we're safer if we stay off the radar. We think the best bet is to keep the boat in the harbor, except, as J.K. Rowling says, "Keeping the boat in the harbor is the only way we can actually fail."

When I wrote my first book, someone close to me was upset. She felt that writing about personal issues and one's family was a betrayal. I was upset that she was upset and I woke up in cold sweats for weeks, thinking what a bad person I was to hurt someone I loved. I should never have written that book, should never have published. What we forget in the fear tornado is the cost of the alternative. If I never wrote the book, then there wouldn't be thousands of people who read the book, who sent emails saying that, after many years, they finally felt hope. I would never have developed the strategies that have helped hundreds of our clients publish bestselling books and make more money than they've ever made before.

When the pandemic shut down my husband's industry for eighteen months, I would never have been able to support my family. I wouldn't have been able to have the honor of being in this conversation with you now. I never would have paid forward the gift that Margaret Bullitt-Jonas gave me in her life-saving book.

So instead of caving to the projections and fears of the people we were never meant to serve from the start, let's release these fears together. Surround yourself with golden light, lift your shoulders into a power pose. This is another destiny moment.

No one is going to beg us to be more visible. No one is going to do this work for us. What gets me over the crest of the fear that arises at each new level, is to ask myself: at the end of my life, will I want to have kept myself back so some people are comfortable and didn't judge me? Or do I want to have played full out? Left everything on the field? Given everything I have inside me for the people for whom I can make a real difference. When I ask this question, my soul always answers: PLAY FULL OUT. ALL IN.

What does your soul say?

Because you're here, and still reading this book, I believe your answer is also to serve, to lead to heal, to uplevel, to be the lighthouse. You're going to act with courage and be the leader you came here to be.

Emerging thought leaders often think they need to slog for years building their social media audience one follower at a time. Send emails every day to your list of one hundred people, most of whom are from your old job or friends from college who will never be your client.

You're here to change lives and you don't have time to build your audience in this slow, linear way. To fast-track your audience build, to 2x, 3x, and then 10X your audience, I offer one primary, paramount strategy. In fact, I could make this chapter one sentence long:

BE OMNIPRESENT by LEVERAGING OTHER PEOPLE'S AUDIENCES.

If you don't want to take years to increase your visibility, start immediately by getting in front of places, businesses, groups, and organizations *with large audiences of your ideal clients.*

You made a start on this practice in the speaking section. Anytime you speak at someone else's group or event, you're employing this strategy. However, this is more we can do to leverage other audiences.

The work is to add to the list you made in the speaking section, adding even more types of places your ideal client or reader engages in life. I call this the ecosystem exercise. We're adding more places your person hangs out, seeks content, spends time, and invests money. We can start this exercise by looking at your ideal client's demographics.

Do they live in certain geographic areas?

Age?

Education?

Hobbies?

Occupation?

Are they married? Have children? Take care of parents? Members of certain community organizations or online memberships?

Also look at their psychographics. Have they experienced a certain type of trauma: war, divorce, infertility, abuse? Or what are their passions? Obsessions?

What are their values and ideals? What are their dreams and hopes? Do they share a common dream like time freedom or working abroad?

Then, what do they spend money on?

Here is an example of the common denominators of many of our Thought Leader Academy clients:

A woman coach or entrepreneur who feels a calling to make a bigger impact than she's currently making. She likes/follows Brené Brown, Glennon Doyle, Mel Robbins, Gabby Bernstein, Michelle Obama. The ultimate media appearance would be on Oprah's Super Soul Sunday. She's obsessed with personal growth and is a lifelong learner. She listens to podcasts like *You Can Do Hard Things, Unblocking Us,* and subscribes to memberships like MindValley. She spends money and has invested in fitness (gym/trainer), self-care (like massage, chiropractor, energy work), she's invested in business or other coaching, she reads self-help books such as *You Are a Badass* by Jen Sincero. She likes travel, particularly retreats and trips that will expand her vibration, creativity, and open her soul. She cares about and puts attention on her environment from her home, to her workspace, to her external environment of community and climate. deep connections with clients and friends. She uses multiple social media platforms (i.e. Facebook, Instagram, Linked In, YouTube). She believes in and works on abundance and money mindset, she likes great food, health products, and will invest in services and products that create her next level.

She knows she's great at what she does and has already achieved results for clients. She knows/feels she "has a book (or likely several) books in her" and while she feels some fears about visibility, experiences a "calling" to share her story/message/mission through speaking, podcasts, TV, etc., but she feels overwhelmed with HOW to expand her impact and accomplish these creative and business dreams.

Her work is a calling, her purpose. She is driven by a vision of making a difference, of truly helping people.

She loves money, but money is not the main goal; it is a result of her living her purpose and making a contribution.

She is motivated, an action taker. Once she has the "play book," the right strategy, she will run with it and be an A-student. She is a visionary, resilient, a servant leader inspired by her passion.

Her greatest fear is that she will leave this life/her work/business without fulfilling her potential, "be a tree falling silently in the forest," that she won't make the ultimate contribution she came to make-to be seen and known-be the leader she came to be. She also fears judgment of others.

Sometimes she feels overwhelmed at the big-ness of her vision.

She feels some self-doubt and unworthiness and fears judgment. She struggles to overcome conditioned, family, society messages of staying small, being in the background, keeping "humble," which is in tension with the calling of her soul to SHINE HER LIGHT.

I can go further and list out all the services my clients ask me to refer them to: marketing/branding strategist, photography/videography for social media or author photos, hair/make-up/style, web/graphic design, financial advising, business attorneys for trademarking and LLC/S-Corp filing. Social media manager, ads manager, event planner, tech and apps like ones that house courses and host online events such as Kajabi, Zoom, and project management software like Asana and Slack.

Clients ask me for referrals to great virtual assistants, project managers, public relations agents, media producers, and editors of magazines. They ask for referrals to nutritionists, functional medicine practitioners, personal trainers, yoga teachers, wellness resort managers, and bookstore owners.

And until we had our own publishing house, they asked me for referrals to publishers, agents, ghostwriters, copyeditors, proofreaders, and book marketers who will work with at least one mindset or energy coach/practitioner. I could add hotel managers, travel agents (to organize retreats), airline miles programs, tickets to industry events.

Why is it useful to have such an extensive understanding of the ideal person I serve? In the BUILD strategy of thought leadership, I understand that I can only support my ideal person if she knows I exist. I can certainly put out content to my initial tiny audience and "hope" she stumbles on my website or is one of the fraction of people on my Instagram account who actually make it through the algorithm and see my post. However, a better option, to be of greatest service, is to meet her where she is. Make it easy. Come to her.

I can only come to her if I know where she is. Every one of those people, places, categories, and services I listed above has an audience. My job, and your job now too, is to find the people, places, organizations with the largest audiences of your ideal person, create a mission bridge with them, and be there with love, inspiration, value, and support plus invitations to go further with you.

We can "be" at these places and in front of these audiences in many ways. As I offer the Thought Leader methods on audience building, I recommend that you pretend we're at a boutique trying on clothes. Try on these different "visibility outfits" and see what you like best, which color looks best, brings out your eyes, and celebrates your gorgeous shape. If you prefer video training to reading about these strategies, you can access my masterclass on the strategies in this section here:

An obvious (and often effective) way to 10X your audience is through running ads. If my ideal person primarily spends time on Instagram and YouTube and I run ads for my masterclasses on those platforms, she has a good chance of seeing my posts. Ads require a marketing budget and can also have a harder time cutting through all the other ads being thrown up at our ideal people online, so I spent the first years (until this year in fact!), until after we'd made $2 million in a year, to run ads. You can run ads immediately, just get someone great who is an expert on the platform you choose to run them for you.

Another way to grow your audience is through public relations. A PR agent or agency can get you visible in top TV, radio, magazine, and online outlets. The key to making this actually grow your audience is to ensure that the outlets where you'll appear are a match to where your ideal person is consuming content. One year, I did a media tour of live TV segments on all the major US networks: ABC, NBC, FOX, CBS, and so on. This is great if my ideal person watches local news, but my ideal client, if they watch the news at all, scans headlines online. The key then was for me to put the segments into social posts along with the network logo and turn the content into valuable teachings on how to choose the right media for your target audience. I also contribute to *Forbes*.

However, I doubt any of my ideal clients read *Forbes* regularly online. To make the *Forbes* articles reach my ideal person, just like with the TV segments, I turn them into posts on my client's favorite platforms and share the article as part of a post on how to get published in national print outlets.

Clients often come to me and say they want to invest in PR to solve their "visibility issue." I tell them what I just shared with you. PR agencies typically require an investment $4,500-$15K per month at the time of writing this book so like running ads, this strategy requires a larger budget, and if applicable, a commitment to leverage your appearances in the spaces where your ideal client consumes information.

Ninety percent of my clients are like I was until earlier this year, amazing leaders who want to find less costly ways of building their audience. If you want to grow your audience "organically," here is the number one Thought Leader Academy way I teach our clients.

One of my mentors, Shanda Sumpter, the founder of Heartcore business, never set out to be a leading expert on audience building. She immigrated from Canada to the US and struggled to find her financial footing in real estate. She even had multiple homes go into foreclosure before innovating a new strategy and becoming a top performer (to the tune of selling over ___ in a year). She brought her superpowers to business coaching and leadership when she saw coaches and entrepreneurs hitting the same wall she'd hit in real estate. "People start in the wrong place," she tells me and her now large audiences of hundreds of thousands. They build websites, launch podcasts, develop elaborate courses and programs, do "marketing," but they don't have any buyers. The strategy that launched her career: build the buyers' list first, ask them what they want, and then give it to them with total generosity and service.

By focusing on building her list first and teaching others to employ her method at her List Power Intensives, Shanda built Heartcore into an eight figure+ a year business.

No one wants to build an email list. In fact, did you groan or lean away from the book when you read the last paragraph? I understand. When I began to train with Shanda, a friend of mine said, "Ick. I'm just going to focus on Facebook." There are many ways to build, AND I will say that by making this my focus like Shanda did, our business grew to multiple seven figures. My colleague reported making $200k. Let me also be clear, some of my clients don't want a big business and income is by no means the only measure of impact or success. I share the numbers simply to say that as much as it's unsexy, un-fun sounding, and seems boring to focus on an email list, there is significant evidence to support that building one, as part of this bigger strategy of BUILD, is worth our time.

Why? Because you own your email list and on social media, you're a renter. The platform can change, go away, delete your account, and adapt algorithms at a whim, disallowing you the ability to ensure that your people see what you post. When you send an email, as long as someone opens it, they'll receive your words, your ideas, your support, your invitations.

This is NOT an either/or proposition. I 100 percent coach our clients to both build an email list AND be engaged and omnipresent on social. But Sara, you might be thinking, what happened to "leverage other people's audiences"? How does building our own email list fit into this strategy?

Enter: THE COLLABORATIVE EVENT.

Here's the first way you can employ this practice: You find people with large audiences of your ideal client and host a joint event online. The event can be any format you like: webinar, masterclass, workshop, retreat, panel, interview series (aka summit), even an in-person event. Your collaborators invite their audience and community. You invite yours. The event is typically free to participants. (Your goal is not immediate income generation; it's expanding your audience.) To attend, however, participants must give their name and email. Everyone who registers becomes part of your email list, your expanded audience.

Compare these scenarios: you host a workshop. You invite people on your social media and email list. If you're just starting to build an audience, maybe thirty people register and five show up live to the workshop. You do the same amount of work creating the content, promoting the event. You have five possible new clients and one or none take a next step with you. That sucks. That's hard.

Now, imagine you create a workshop and invite five people who do different services than you do, but what they offer is one of those services you identified earlier in which your ideal person invests. They invite hundreds or thousands of their clients, you invite your community, and now one thousand people register for the workshop and over one hundred attend live. You follow up with these new beautiful one hundred people and ten of them invest with you. How does that feel? Instead of spending years building your audience up to thousands, you shared audiences with these other leaders. The audience found more of what they need all in one place. Your collaborators got in front of many new people and attracted new clients. You attracted ten new clients and grew your email list by close to one thousand people without paying a cent in ads. WIN-WIN-WIN.

You'll enroll collaborators to do events with you the same way you book speaking engagements. You can use that same six-step pitch I taught you in the SPEAK chapter. Simply adapt "be a guest on your event/show" to an invitation to joint host an event. Acknowledge their awesomeness as a leader, build a mission bridge based on your values and the shared person you both serve, describe your vision for the event, and let them know how easy it will be to participate. To get even more YESs, offer to host the event on your platform, write the email and social media posts they can send to invite their audience, and give them the best choice of times to present. When we come from generosity and service, miracles happen. Everyone wins.

Here's another type of collaborative event: STRATEGIC PARTNERSHIPS.

As with a collaborative event, a strategic partnership is based on the idea of creating WIN-WIN-WINS. A strategic partnership, however, does not necessitate cohosting an event. A strategic partnership could take place in many forms including:

An expert or organization could send an email to their large list promoting your work, service, or event, and in return, you would do the same when they launch a new product, book, or other event later in the year.

An expert or organization could send an email to their large list promoting your work, and in return, you give a workshop for free at their organization. (Yes, this is also a speaking engagement.)

A strategic partner could promote your services to their community and audience, and you'd offer them a referral fee for each person who invests with you or joins your course. (This is also called an affiliate relationship or referral partner.) Marie Forleo built her eight-figure empire and now famous course, B-School, using this as her primary strategy.

Although NBC or another network wouldn't use the term strategic partner, I consider it a strategic partnership when you appear as topic expert in a regular segment on a show and the show promotes you and your work on their program and website.

Strategic partnerships have so much potential and are so rewarding, I developed an entire training on Strategic Partnerships for our Thought Leader clients. At the nucleus of the training is an idea you'll recognize from earlier sections of this book: to attract amazing strategic partners, focus first on creating the WIN for the partner. Joe Polish made this his main goal in building the global Genius Network and relationships with industry giants like Richard Branson and the president of Hay House. His mantra (inspired I believe by Zig Zigler), to get what you want, help other people achieve what they want. Just like in speaking pitching, we make our first outreach(es) ABOUT THEM. The odd paradox here is that we don't focus on other people to GET a certain result. The magic happens when we focus on them freely, without attachment to any outcome or return. We trust that somehow, some way, the good energy will circulate, but we make no expectations or demands. In my experience, when we focus entirely on helping others get what they want, our needs are met, often exceeded, and often in surprising ways.

Here are ten ways you can begin to create positive connections with those with whom you want to strategic partner:

If they have a book, write a five-star review on Amazon. (Email them directly or send a DM to their team on social media and say how much you love the book and share the screenshot of the review.)

Buy their book for your clients and let their team know you've decided to make the book your welcome gift for your people.

Subscribe to, positive review, and share their podcast. (Same as above with the book, take a screenshot of the review and tag them in the post you make shouting out their show.)

Repost their content. (Even leaders with huge platforms seek engagement. It's a true help to them for other people to reshare, comment on, and tell others about their work.)

Attend or volunteer at the events hosted by the person or organization.

Promote and bring groups to the event put on by the person or organization.

Donate to the favorite charity or cause of the person or organization.

One year I tried to develop a relationship with a big health organization that put on women's events in Chicago. I applied online to be a presenter and was declined. I really liked the organization and had heard great things about their events, so I went in person to their head office and submitted another application. The head of the event told me they had already chosen speakers, and I really wasn't a "big enough name" to be featured. I took a few huge swallows to bring down the lump of shame in my throat. "No problem!" I said. "How else could I help?" She tapped her fingers on her desk and shrugged. She was busy and clearly I was an annoyance between her and the to-do list. "Never mind," I said and, sweating through my shirt, handed her the glossy white folder of my materials, bio, and pitch I'd assembled. I imagined this would go straight in the trash when I left the office, but while I'd waited to speak with her, I'd overheard two of the employees say the event wasn't selling as quickly as they hoped.

"I'll start promoting your event at the organizations I'm part of," I told her. "I'll bring a group and we'll all buy tickets." She shrugged about that and I left. I didn't have a huge group of people to buy tickets, but I vowed to find people. I talked to my yoga teacher, invited my clients, and bought tickets for a few friends. Six weeks before the event, I received a phone call from the woman I'd pitched at the office. I didn't recognize her voice, and several months had passed and I didn't recognize her last name. "Are you still available?" she asked. "One of our presenters dropped out. I found your folder in my desk drawer." I took the stage to my biggest audience to date the next month.

One of our Thought Leader clients had a similar experience with this practice. Her goal was to work with Fortune 1000 companies, top universities, and women in tech. Instead of cold pitching the HR departments of companies, she offered to host her university reunion reception. She stayed an extra day where the university was hosting a conference with leaders from several companies in Silicon Valley with which she wanted to partner. She found the event organizer and volunteered to set up chairs in the breakout rooms. She met a woman from one of the companies who was hosting a big conference. My client signed up for that conference, arrived early, and helped the organizers set up the flowers, ensure the gift bags were beautifully displayed. An hour into the opening reception, one of the organizers rushed by her in a panic. "Our workshop leader can't make it. Her flight is grounded." The organizer looked at my client. "There isn't any way you would . . ." My client presented to three hundred people and was invited to the banquet dinner with the headline speakers and CEO of the company. A few months later, that company asked if she'd take on their top six women executives as coaching clients. Since then, she's signed six-figure coaching contracts with companies, been paid up to $30K for keynotes, even $15K for keynotes on zoom from her home.

She started by setting up chairs.

Another of our clients with a similar vision and who'd just booked at $20K keynote, came and spoke to our new thought leaders earlier this year. "To get the BIG strategic partnerships, you have to be willing to play the long game."

I teach our thought leaders a strategic partner game called Apples and Orchards. Make a list of accessible strategic partners. These would be people you know, or someone you know well knows, or organizations you don't have any connection to that are at a level of business and visibility within the same or double of yours. So, if you run a six-figure business and have 10K followers on social media, then businesses in the six-figure range with a similar audience size for example. These are your apples.

Then list the top five BIG strategic partners. People or organizations with 10X or more the reach than you have currently. These are your orchards. Every week, reach out to at least three apples and ask them their number one goal for the year and how you can support them. If they ask you how they can support you, propose a partnership idea. Or focus on serving them for a little while, and then propose. Also each week, take one relationship building action toward one of your orchards. Use the list above for ideas such as post a review, promote their latest endeavor, set up chairs at their event.

Relationships will deepen. Partnerships will happen. Abundance will come.

CHAPTER EIGHT

Monetize Your Mission

CONGRATULATIONS! You've come far in your thought leader journey! The terrific truth is that after publishing your writing, speaking on virtual and live stages and shows, and starting to build an ever expanding audience, you have visibility, credibility, and impact! Wooo-hooo! However, as you recall from chapter one, you may still not be making the income you desire, that you deserve!

To start matching the money you want with the world-changing mission you're on, we start with a vision. You've likely heard the adage from Proverbs:

Without Vision, the people perish.

When I started life as an entrepreneur, I didn't have a clear, big vision, and I certainly didn't use the word entrepreneur or think of myself that way. I was a writer! A coach! A creative! I felt repelled by any training, book, or class that used words like funnel, pipeline, and sales.

I offered sessions one at a time, never promoted myself, never asked for referrals. I knew and learned nothing about creating programs or packages or scaling my work to serve groups.

At the beginning, I offered women's empowerment life coaching and, in what felt like a completely separate area of my life, a writer. I loved both aspects of my work. When clients came to me for coaching (I can hardly believe anyone found me), I offered the deepest work, based on years of training in mind-body, quantum physics, spirituality. I was deeply and fully present with my clients. The work produced results, sometimes tremendous and surprising results. I was coaching from my soul. I thought my strategy was a good one. Do the deepest, most excellent, powerful work. Serve whoever the universe sends.

A few years (yes, years plural) into this work, I met with an accountant to file my taxes. We met in person in his office in a dense old Art Deco building on a dark stretch of Madison in the Chicago loop. The building was populated with law offices, therapy practices, and accountants. "The good news," he said, typing away, head bowed, at his keyboard, "is you'll owe almost nothing to the IRS." This was good news. "Wow," he paused and for the first time, looked at me. "You really don't make much money."

Shame stabbed my chest. I wanted to be angry at the accountant. Or my husband for saying my career was like playing the craps table in Vegas. He was referring more to the book publishing part of my work, but either way, according to the accountant, I had no business to speak of. I'd made $20,000 that year.

Clients have come to me in similar pain. "I don't want a hobby," they say. "I want a business." But we don't "count" our work often as successful unless it's producing a certain financial return. We want the financial abundance WITH the fulfillment of knowing we are bringing excellence and our genius to our clients. We say we want it, our conscious minds do want it. But there are other parts, often subconscious parts, that wave big "NOOO, NOOO, NOOO" signs every time we put another "six-figure year!" on our vision boards.

I stomped out of the accountant's office. I wanted to be angry at society and the inequality in women's pay and my mother for saying, "you're not good with money." (I wasn't.) I wanted to be angry at everyone close to me who "didn't believe in me."

"Who doesn't believe in you?" the therapist with whom I was working on all that childhood sex abuse trauma at the time asked me in our next session.

I stared at him, seething.

"You're talking about your husband, the accountant, your family, society . . . and my question is WHO, really, doesn't believe in you?"

"Me," I answered. It felt true that none of those other people or groups believed in me either, but the truth was, I had no trust in myself. I had no faith in my ability to create financial abundance. "I don't believe in me," I said.

I didn't believe in myself, but I did understand that if I kept doing what I was doing, I would end up in that accountant's office next December having the precise conversation, saturating in shame, with around $20,000 in income for the year. Resonance came over me. I could feel myself at a destiny moment, at the choice point in the road. I decided to take my victim thinking, the trauma effects (one of which was chronic undervaluing myself and underearning), and all the lack, money negative, limiting beliefs I'd been lugging around in a hundred pound backpack-to take it all head on and CHANGE. I vowed to go ALL IN, to leave no stone unturned. This wasn't about money anymore; it was a spiritual mandate to break poverty, unworthiness, and lack off my family and hopefully, by doing so, become a space where other women, artists, coaches, healers, entrepreneurs, and leaders could do the same.

I knew this transformation was not going to be subtle. I could feel that, like recovering from an addiction or summiting a high mountain, it would require radical new thinking, behaviors, habits, and action. What I found is that it required an uplevel of my identity. I went for this work from every possible direction, investing in coaching, mindset work, spiritual practice, new styles of meditation, neuroscience techniques.

I thought often of what Hemingway says about writing, "Writing is easy. Just open a vein, and bleed." Transforming lack to abundance when you come from where I came from is an alchemical, full body-mind-spirit experience. Transmutation of old ideas, agreements, and patterns, many of them ancestral and epigenetic. Then transformation of my present-day life.

That next year was the first time I broke the six-figure mark as a coach. $120K. The next year, I made $250K. We've (it's we now because I work with a team!), doubled every year since, last year hitting $2M in sales.

Have you had an experience like mine in the accountant's office? Do you know in your soul that you are capable of more, deserve more, are worth more, and want more? Do you also feel other parts of you questioning your worth, capability, and value?

If so, keep reading so I can show you everything I did to change my financial destiny, my worth identity, to make more money than I imagined I could, and help my clients in Thought Leader Academy do the same.

In November of 2021, I tripped on a raised section of sidewalk and scraped my arm as I hit the cement. I tripped because (yes, I was looking at my phone), where I'd received an email with a study from Oxfam that reported women had lost $800 billion dollars in the global Covid pandemic. I was certain the study must contain a type. Surely they mean $800 million, which is hardly better, but perhaps not quite as catastrophic.

Nope. The figure was correct. $800 BILLION.

I called my friend and accountability buddy, Molly Jones. "It's not like we needed another setback," I said. Even in 2021, I knew women made between $0.65-.80 to the dollar as male colleagues and as I shared in Chapter two, even women freelancers made 28 percent less than their equally qualified male counterparts.

"I'm sick of it," I said.

"What are you going to do about it?" she said.

I understood I was not going to single-handedly solve the women's economic crisis, hardly make a dent, but I also understood I was either part of the problem, or I could be part of the solution.

I went home and pulled out all the prosperity and finance books I'd worked with over the past years, books that helped me move from that day in the accountant's office, struggling to make $20,000/year as a writer and coach to making over $1M year doing the same services. *Think and Grow Rich, Attracting Money, Creating Money: Attracting Abundance, You Are a Badass at Making Money, Spiritual Economics*, and *The Science of Getting Rich*, by Wallace Wattles.

"I could pull the best techniques from all of these and teach a free online workshop," I texted Molly. "I want a new book though. I want *The Science of Getting Rich, for Women."*

"On Amazon, looking," Molly texted back. I raced her to the search bar. We couldn't find that book.

"Better get writing," Molly texted.

The result of this vow to be some part of the solution was my book *The Science of Getting Rich for Women*, and if you read that book, many of the abundance generating practices here will be familiar. I've included some new techniques and practices here also because I continue to do abundance work daily and discover new strategies regularly as I go.

One note, as we ascend toward this next thought leader summit, this work will be both internal and external. If you're not already making the full financial abundance you desire, you will likely come up against subconscious resistance, old family agreements, ancestral patterns, cultural programming, effects of past traumas, all kinds of things. I'm going to include ways for you to navigate, dissolve, and liberate yourself from this resistance, to help you align all the parts of you so you can have what you really deserve, which is massive abundance.

Now, finally, we'll get to your Abundance Vision.

Let's go back to that thought leader magic wand. If you could make any amount of money through your writing, speaking, programs, and products per year, what would that amount be?

[Side note: writing down a goal has been proven to increase the likelihood of the fulfillment of that goal to about 80 percent likelihood versus a 20 percent likelihood if we just think about that number. That's a huge jump just by writing it down. So congratulations on being 80 percent likely to achieve your goal. By the end of this section, I'll show you how to be at 100 percent.]

Now answer, how would you like this money to come to you:
- Book sales
- Paid speaking
- clients
- Students in course
- Retreats
- Workshops
- Group membership
- Other?

Once you determine the ways you'd like abundance to come, it can be powerful to imagine your ideal client or reader PATHWAY. The me years ago in the accountant's office didn't know how important it was to give myself and the universe a "mold," a pathway to fill. When we think "one off" vs program or a single product, versus pathway, we limit the number of people we can serve and the depths and heights to which we can serve them. We also limit our abundance.

Your pathway is the ultimate journey your ideal client will take with you. If someone starts by taking your masterclass, then enrolls in a six-week course, then your year-long membership, and then, for the ideal, right fit people, your $25K one-on-one coaching program.

It's powerful to create a visual picture of this pathway, to remind yourself what you're creating, and to share it with your incoming clients to inspire them about the journey ahead. Play with images that inspire you.

MONETIZE YOUR MISSION

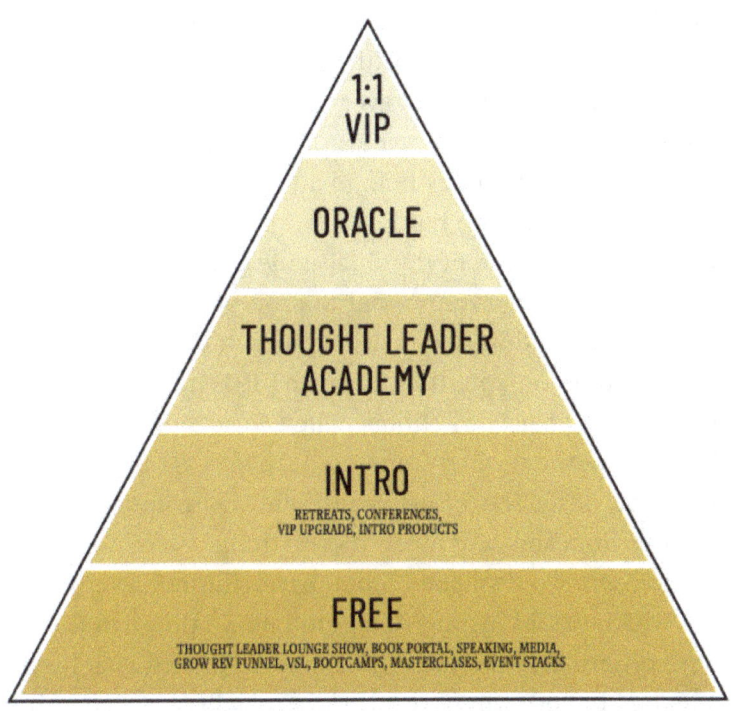

saraconnell.com

You can draw an ascension pyramid, a winding path, a pie chart. The above graphic shows my client pathway the year we took the business over $1M.

Next, answer, WHY is this abundance and your client offerings important to you? When I smashed my first financial glass ceiling, it was important to me to break lack/unworthiness off my female family line and to be a coach and offer a space for my clients to make first hundreds of thousands and then millions of dollars.

Answer: What's different and better in your life when you're bringing in that amount per year?

Who else benefits (family, friends, clients)?

How is the world better when you are making this amount of abundance?

We spend time doing this inquiry before taking revenue-producing actions because we want to align with the sacredness of your desire, the way you having more will benefit everyone. We want to begin to illuminate and dissolve the false ideas we've picked up from society, religion, family, the media about money being bad or limiting, false ideas that if we have more, someone else has less.

If you've taken on some of those false ideas about abundance, a fun exercise is to write a huge number at the top of the page. Five million, $10 million, $100 million. Then list what you'd do with the money. Where/how would you spend or invest it? I've never seen one of my clients write a list of greedy things. They write how they'll buy their dream home, a new car, take some epic trips, AND they start foundations, give generously, share the wealth, and contribute to causes and people about whom the care. Even if everything you write is something for you personally, you'd still be modeling worthiness, ability, and financial power, which would inspire others to believe they can do the same. After doing intensive abundance transformation and coaching for the past five years, I believe when we "win" financially, everyone wins.

Once we've aligned with the sacredness of our abundance goal, the next step is to expand your Monetize Your Mission list. Keep exploring fun ways you'd love money to come to you. Would you like the money to come through volume book sales by companies that also ask you to come and speak? Podcasts or book tour sponsors? Corporate coaching, consulting, products, courses? International retreats? If you want more ideas, a high vibe exercise is to take a week and write down every time you see someone making money in a way that excites you and inspires you. Do they have a brick and mortar store and sell something? Are they an online expert? Do they need to get paid to come in and give a presentation at Google?

Now that you have a list of the ways you'd love the money to come to you, let's dial in the vision even further. Like going from general speaking categories, "I'd like to speak at not-for-profit groups with over one hundred employees," and then making a spreadsheet of one hundred specific company names, you'll now make a chart, spreadsheet, or diagram of the number you'd like to receive from each of those "ways" of earning income.

For example, one of our Thought Leader clients came to me last year and said she wanted to make $1milllon, but didn't want to run groups, have a team, or be tied to a thirty-hour per week coaching schedule. Her chart had one line item: coach ten clients at $100K each.

Another client said, "I want to give quarterly paid workshops and then have people from those workshops join my online course." She wanted to make $250K for the year. Her spreadsheet had two line items:

- Quarterly workshops, twenty people each quarter, so sixty each year, paying $997 per workshop. That gives her just under $60K.
- Course generating $190K at $3K per course participant = sixty-three people enrolling in the course.

These two offerings = $250K year.

For our $2 million year, we had seven offerings:

- Thought Leader Academy
- Oracle (or advanced Thought Leader Mastermind)
- Coaching and VIP Days (I work with five leaders one-on-one at a time)
- Paid workshops, intensives and The Science of Getting Rich Abundance Accelerator
- Paid speaking
- Book sales
- Black Friday bestselling book bundle

When you have a vision of the income you want to receive, and have specified the way you'd love the money to come to you, you'll accelerate the speed at which it arrives. Even if the money doesn't come exactly in the way you envision now, the specificity and your alignment and action towards your vision will bring in the abundance in mighty and powerful ways.

If you don't feel crystal glass clear yet, keep your eyes open to the exciting ways other leaders are monetizing their missions. Remember the Thought Leader agreement: I am one with that. It can be tempting to look at other people and think, *Oh it's easy for them but can't happen for me.* Our brain will want to see differences, to separate. I offer to flip that old pattern and instead say, "I would only see this if it's here for me too. The very fact that I saw this post on Instagram or in my email inbox or on the Starbuck's bulletin board is because it's my inspiration, my 'sneak preview.' What I'm seeking is seeking me."

Now you can get excited to see someone with a million Facebook followers. You can get curious: how did they do that? DM to ask or read interviews they give or listen to their guest appearances on podcasts. Write down what they did. Use their roadmap.

Remember that neither or 98 percent of any of our Thought Leader Academy clients had any social media, email list, or celebrity connections when we started. I just kept taking one step at a time, learning the strategies that you're learning in this book and others like it, putting them into action, and building a step at a time.

This vision work can bring up gremlins. In fact, if the number you wrote brought up any for you, let's celebrate. The gremlins only arise if you're serious about transforming your financial destiny, if that glass ceiling is going to be smashed!

If/when any lack, comparison, judgment, or gremlins come up, here is an exercise I do that shifts my energy in a big way. I've written it here or you can also download it here:

Use the worksheet or create four columns on a blank journal page or screen.

Column I: Write the number you want to receive this year.

Column II: Write ALL the reasons your gremlins say you can't have that number. No being spiritual here. Just let your inner critic, saboteur, head gremlin list every fear, limiting belief, past failure, message from childhood. Get it out.

Column III: Write the opposite of each of the gremlin statements. For example: I've never been able to make six figures becomes, I now easily generate over six figures a year through work I love. You don't need to believe the column III statement, just write the opposite.

Column IV: How you'd transform or solve the fear. You can ask your future self, "How did I solve this?" or pretend a great friend called in the same situation and asked your advice.

Example: Column II: I don't have time to pursue this new work. Column IV: I get up one hour earlier, three days/week, and hire a babysitter every Thursday 4-6:00 p.m., giving myself five full hours a week to devote fully to my vision.

Or Column II: I've never done this before and don't believe it will work for me. Column IV: Interview or read about ten people who've done this and list the common denominators-the things they all did. Follow this roadmap by taking one action per day that they did to achieve this goal. Add five minutes of BELIEVE meditation to my day. Breathe in, I CAN, breath out, I WILL.

Just like with column III, you don't need to believe the actions will work; simply list what a person in your situation COULD do to solve/transform it.

One more exciting thing to consider: the ONLY thing standing in the way of you and your awesome, amazing, prosperous ABUNDANCE number is what you wrote in Column II.

Your mind will tell you it's the economy, your family, your past, your education, your background, your intelligence, what your third grade teacher or your sister or your Dad thought about you. But research shows it's only the subconscious resistance that has to change.

The transformer exercise you just did will take you far. I want those beliefs GONE for you. I want you to smash every glass ceiling at every level as you ascend to your full financial abundance. So, in *The Science of Getting Rich for Women*, I introduced the magic equation to creating real, big, and lasting abundance through our thought leadership.

BE + RELEASE + DO = HAVE

BE is the vision. Defining the number and embodying and expressing the identity of someone receiving that kind of abundance. Moving through your day AS the bestselling author, $20K keynote speaker, six- or seven-figure CEO.

RELEASE is the step we just took. Identifying those resistant beliefs, those lack mindsets, and dissolving them at a subconscious level. I urge you to use the neuroscience modalities at the Thought Leader book portal here:

Whew!

You're ready! You're moving to the third part of the magic equation: DO. This is the action step. It's time for the *Science of Getting Rich for Women* ABUNDANCE ACCELERATOR!

The Abundance Accelerator is a one-month course I run once or twice a year to help our Thought Leader Academy clients take big leaps in revenue generation in a short period of time. Every time we've run the course, the group of about twenty leaders has generated over $1 million in new income!

We've had clients make more in the accelerator than they had in the entire previous year. I'm going to walk you through the accelerator step-by-step so you can make a terrific leap in the next four weeks. Yes, the power of doing the accelerator in the group helps tremendously, AND, the action steps are the action steps. Like the person who eats less processed food and empty calories plus adds an hour of exercise four days a week will release weight and transform their health, anytime we take abundance generating actions, we WILL generate more abundance. You can access the Abundance Accelerator workbook here:

One member of the first class of Thought Leader Academy, a badass leader specializing in coaching women in corporate jobs, has done the accelerator every time we've run it. In her second round, she set a wild goal for herself to generate $50K. She generated $69K and went on to have her highest income year to date.

We have participants who've never received money for their thought leadership get their first big client. Clients who were in a three-month slump made six figures in four weeks. Every time I lead the accelerator, the income in our company jumps.

The Abundance Accelerator is designed to create the breakthrough you need. Sometimes I've been in a place of not knowing what to do to create more abundance. Other times, I've known what to do, but I've felt such extreme resistance to being in action. Until we can be together online or in a room doing the accelerator live, I'm going to give you the crash course and the complete roadmap to have a major financial breakthrough here.

Abundance Accelerator Roadmap

Step One: VISION

If you can see it, you can achieve it.

Write the $ amount you'd like to receive in the next four weeks. (You can also set a longer term goal of ninety days or between now and the end of the year.)

Step Two: MINDSET

The only thing that could stand in your way are subconscious limiting beliefs.

Remember you can use the four columns exercise I described in an earlier section along with the neuroscience release modalities:

The exercise will release and transform any limiting ideas about your ability to receive this number and have a big breakthrough in monetizing your mission. Continue using these techniques throughout the accelerator.

Step Three: YOUR OFFER

You can monetize ANYTHING.

Identify the ways you'd like to receive the increased income.

If you already have a business, service, or product, choose the offer you'd like to focus on for the accelerator. For example, if you have a fourteen-day jump start, a six-month coaching program, and a one-on-one year-long coaching program, decide which you enjoy most, have had the most interest in, and which will most quickly increase your abundance. If you love the six-month program but know it will require time and tech support to set up the logistics, you could focus on attracting one new one-on-one client per week, increase the cash flow, and invest in the six-month group prep and launch as phase II. Alternatively, if you're full with one-on-one clients and want to scale with a group, make the entire focus on the accelerator outreach on and filling the first ten spots in your six-month group program.

If you do not already offer programs or products or you don't feel clear of the best offer to focus on for the accelerator, play the Fifty WAYS game.

Fifty WAYS

Set a timer for twenty minutes. Without censoring yourself, in the energy of a brainstorm, write every possible way you can think of to generate the amount of money you desire. You don't have to be willing to do the things you write. Try asking: "If someone with my skill set and experience was going to create this amount of money, they would ___" and write down what ideas flow. Your goal is fifty ideas. Keep going to the finish line. If you need more time, take it.

To help create possibilities, you can think of every service that you or people you know invest in. Then write any of those services you are capable of providing on your fifty ways list.

You can also list any passions or hobbies you have that people may want to learn or experience. I've had clients turn their passion into guided bike tours in other countries, curated networking events, paid masterclasses, cooking tutorials, real estate investments, and week-long retreats.

One of our thought leader clients wanted to add another stream of income to fund international travel she was excited to do. She played the Fifty Ways game and realized she loved having people stay in her home. She loved creating beautiful, sacred spaces. She organized her house into a stunning sanctuary. Then she listed the house on several vacation rental sites. She's so far this year made $45K from renting her home while she traveled to Europe, London, Mexico, and soon she'll be leading a group of clients on a transformation retreat to Egypt.

If you already know your offers/programs/services, you can still play Fifty Ways to generate creative and exciting new possibilities for marketing, scaling, and increasing your abundance.

> *"The money we desire is already here in the form of an opportunity not yet actioned."*
> Fabienne Fredrickson

The goal of Fifty Ways is to reveal the abundance of ways the money can come to you and give you an action list.

Once you've generated fifty ideas, highlight the ones that feel:

- Easiest
- Most immediately lucrative/actionable
- Fun/exciting

Eliminate any you're not willing to do or that don't feel aligned. For example, once I wrote "sell car" on my Fifty Ways list. Selling my car could generate money, but I also use my car daily to pick up my son, get groceries, and other tasks important to running my house. I crossed off "sell car" and focused on the actions that involved networking, referrals, and guest speaking on topics related to my business.

Next, put your "yes"/highlighted actions in priority order. Take action on one at a time until you reach your financial goal.

One November, I was $200K away from my abundance goal for the year. I played Fifty Ways and hated forty-five of the fifty ideas I generated. My well felt dry and I could not see a way to our goal number. Only because I couldn't think of anything better, I took action on the five ideas that seemed okay. As it does with the Fifty Ways game, magic was ignited. Not a single one of my initial five ideas produced abundance, but while I took those actions, a friend invited me to a networking group where I met ten new clients! Ten! I also got inspired on a walk during the time of onboarding those clients and thought of an end-of-year workshop that led to a new coaching offer. By December 20, when I stopped work for the holidays, we'd generated another $240K in sales.

Every time I've played this game, I've increased my cash flow within a week. Every time.

Step Four: SET UP FOR SUCCESS

You could spend the rest of your accelerator actioning your Fifty Ways ideas. OR you can take your top idea(s) from your Fifty Ways list, and choose one main product/program or service to focus on for the next four weeks.

If you choose something that you've offered and sold successfully already, skip to step five.

If you don't already have an established offer, or you want to focus on something new from Fifty Ways, the next step is some speedy market research. Identify three-ten people who represent the exact kind of person you'd like to serve. I.e. people who eat keto, stay-at-home dads, seven-figure entrepreneurs, women who've been diagnosed with rheumatoid arthritis, entrepreneurs focused on improving climate change.

Schedule calls/Zooms/meetings with each of them individually to find out what they want most right now and get feedback on your offer/pricing.

The point of these calls is not to make a sale, although this could happen! The purpose is to be in generous service to them and to get feedback on your offer.

Here's how you can make the invitation: To invite them to the short meeting, say that you'd like to support their number one goal for the year and to get feedback about a new product/program/service you plan to create. Share that your intention is to learn from an amazing person like them—the kind of person you'd like to serve in your work. Share that your intention is for the conversation to be useful to them and that you're excited to support their vision any way you can.

Here is a template for how you can structure the call/Zoom or meeting:

A. What is their number one goal/vision/dream right now? (Get specific; let them feel it, and share why it's important to them.)
B. What is their biggest challenge to achieving that goal? What is it costing them not to have attained it?
C. Share your idea/program/product and ask what they think of it. Would they invest in something like this? Why or why not? What would a program/product of this kind need for them to be interested in investing in it? For what rate?
D. Ask what you can do to help them achieve their number one goal right now and immediately help in any authentic way you can.
E. Invite them to introduce you to anyone who could benefit from what you are doing or could be interested in your new program/service.
F. BONUS: provide them an easy "done for you" email introduction that they can share with people, so it makes it easy for them to share with others who you are and what you do. Send this to them within twenty-four hours of your meeting, along with taking any action you can to support their vision.

My clients sometimes get nervous when I suggest this practice. "What if I don't have a way to help them?" they ask. "What if I don't have any valuable connections for them!" We don't have to spend money or have a celebrity network to support someone else's goals. Find out exactly what they need and ask the universe how you could authentically help.

Here are ways I've supported those I've interviewed at these types of meetings:

- Given them a five-star book review on Amazon
- Subscribed to their podcast
- Retweeted or shared one of their posts
- Referred a client who needed their service or product
- Sent them an encouraging email about reaching their goal
- Visualized their success every morning for one week
- Introduced them to a guest for their podcast
- Promoted their podcast, book, or social media content
- Have them as a guest on my shows/retreats
- Introduced them to a conference organizer who can hire them to speak at the next event
- Shared information about a networking group that might be a great fit for them to meet new clients

As we discussed in the last chapter, almost everyone is seeking more visibility, so supporting or promoting their work to anyone you know would likely be very welcome.

You can also do something personal (non-career) related to support them. If they love their dog and the dog starts suffering from anxiety and you know a holistic dog healer, make an introduction.

You can send them a favorite book, a link to a podcast interview, or YouTube video they might enjoy, if a shared love of art, literature, or mystery novels comes up. Listen closely for anything they love and do something that connects them to that thing!

Step Five: MONETIZE

Through the first four steps, you have a product, program, or service to offer and you have "validated" that offer by receiving feedback. Make adjustments based on any market research you did and now it's time to take that invitation into the field!

In the most recent round of the Abundance Accelerator, the group committed to making an offer per day for six weeks. I had never done this practice personally and was excited to try it.

Like the Power 100 practice, the "offer a day" gives us structure, consistency, and momentum. To get maximum results in monetizing your mission, I recommend trying this for at least a week, ideally thirty days.

An obstacle for so many of the leaders I coach is that they're not making the money they want in part because they're not making enough invitations. I can track my revenue proportionally with the number of offers I make. More invitations = more income.

Here's a way I coach our clients to connect with the ideal people for their daily offers:

Top Ten Lists

Make a list of ten people or organizations you would love to have refer others to your business/service (individuals who lead or know groups of your ideal client).

Make a list of ten people you would love to work with (direct potential clients).

(If you've already been doing your service/offer), make a list of ten people you have worked with previously (whom you loved).

The combination of all three groups becomes your "Love" list!

Group one becomes your "Relationship Development" list.

Group two becomes your "Heart" list.

Group three becomes your "Connect and Invite" list.

How to Reach Out

Our Thought Leader Academy group all raised their hands at this step. "What do I say or do when I reach out to the people on these lists?!"

Here's what I do:

For the Relationship Development list: Do one action/week or month that supports them and helps them achieve their goals. (Examples:

Five-star review of book or podcast that you take a screenshot of and share with them, comment or like a post, send a gift, contribute to their cause/organization, attend their event, bring others to their event.)

For the Heart list: Reach out with a resource, "thinking about you" email or video, or do something that helps them achieve their vision and/or authentically affirms their work/contribution. Invite them to an event or call with you. Pour into them. When it feels right, invite them to a conversation to discuss working with you. If they've already expressed interest but have a concern (money, time, etc.), offer a solution plus a special bonus to start.

For your Connect and Invite list: Same as your Heart list. Send a "thinking about you" email or video, do something that helps them achieve their vision, and/or authentically affirms their work/contribution. Invite them to an event or call with you. Pour into them. Invite them to a call to ask how they're doing, find out how you could help them next, and invite them to introduce you to someone in their world who could benefit from your services.

Story Time

I felt very afraid to reach out to previous clients. I only chose people I adored working with for this list and I respected and valued their time. I worried I would feel pushy or the email would seem like an unwelcome sales pitch versus a genuine love connection. To get over the fear, I decided to create a new service. I wanted the email to be 100 percent authentic and for me that would only happen when I had something real and new to share with them. My email went something like this:

> Hi [insert name of beloved client]
>
> I've been thinking about you and would love to hear how everything is going! Working with you was a highlight of last year and I am so excited (though not surprised!) that your book won the indie book award and that you are now a number one bestselling author.

I'm creating a new VIP coaching program that will help mission driven experts and entrepreneurs write and publish a bestselling book and give a TEDx talk. It's much like what you and I did together but for people who don't have time for a group coaching program but want the big added credibility and visibility to be seen as an industry leader. Because I loved working with you so much, I wanted to share this with you in the event you have other colleagues, clients, or friends who would like this special service. Thank you in advance for anyone you feel inspired to introduce. I would be tremendously honored to support anyone in your world make the impact they are here to make. Regardless, I am so happy to have had the opportunity to connect with you and would be thrilled to set up a Zoom or call to hear your updates-know you are on fire!!

Much love,

Sara

I sent that email to ten beloved previous clients on a Monday morning. By Wednesday, one previous client had made a referral. But the thing that shocked me was that three of the ten said they wanted the new VIP service. They wanted to write another book and do a TEDx talk. I had no intention of any of those clients doing more work with me at that time. But something lit a spark. The single action generated an immediate $65K in new income with exponentially more from referrals over the next weeks and months.

What if you don't have previous clients or aren't totally sure what you want to "offer"?

If that is the case, do not fear.

If you have not attracted a new client/customer yet or are not sure if what you are offering is what your ideal client/customer wants, go to step one again and make your entire focus having one-on-one interviews with people who fit your ideal client profile.

Follow the steps to make the conversation valuable for them and ask direct questions about anything you're considering offering. Get feedback on the service, the investment cost, and what would make it a yes or no for them and why.

Adapt your offer so it (1) matches what they say they want and (2) is authentic for you to provide. Write down or record (with permission) their exact words, and use these in your marketing, outreach, and conversations moving forward.

Research where the kind of person you want to serve hangs out (online or in person) and become visible at those places.

Once you identify your ideal client and where you can find them, use the one offer a day structure to keep in powerful action and increase revenue fast.

One of our Thought Leader clients was in a busy time during the last Abundance Accelerator. Instead of trying to do EVERYTHING in the roadmap, she chose one strategy. She liked the email letter I sent out to previous clients. She copied the exact letter I included in this section and switched the words to be about her business and new program.

She sent the email to a small group of previous clients. Within twenty-four hours, she'd generated over $50K in new business. She sent another round of emails a few weeks later. That one action, sending versions of that one email has generated over six figures of income for her this year.

Let's do a check-in: what actions have you taken so far in the accelerator?

How did it go?

Sometimes, as you take new, big, courageous action, particularly if we don't manifest our desired results instantly, new fears and resistance emerge. As you move through the actions in the Abundance Accelerator, keep checking in with the Science of Getting Rich for Women Magic Equation:

BE + RELEASE + DO = HAVE

BE

When you get up in the morning, are you dressing as your fully monetized, actualized Thought Leader self?

DO

Are you taking the actions your abundant, highly successful Thought Leader self takes?

If not yet, what gets to be released so you can be and do your full vision?

Have any unseen fears surfaced as you thought about or started to take action?

When I first took real action to create a six-figure income year, I discovered a huge fear that making more money and focusing on my business would mean I would be a bad mother and wife. I feared I would lose focus and attention on my son and he would suffer for it.

To release this fear, I met with moms I admired who also had successful businesses. I asked them how they created time for their family while running the business. I saw that while they did give attention to their businesses, they also were present and supportive parents and partners. I saw that in addition, they were modeling empowerment and contribution to their children, something I wanted to do for my son.

The truth is, I now believe as an entrepreneur, I'm a better partner, a better mother. And I'm certainly able to contribute to my family in a way that I never could before I grew my income. I've been able to give my husband the gift of financial support and space to pursue what brings him joy, a gift he gave me years ago and to reciprocate feels incredible. My son sees a woman who is strong, who is committed, is devoted to her craft and calling. He sees a woman who has agency, a woman who knows her voice matters. A woman who's willing to be a stand for the voices of others and make a positive impact in the world. Unlike many generations of men in our family, he sees that both women and men create visions that are important and valuable. I've taken him on book tour, to conferences, and last month to London and Paris. And I still get to drive my son home from school, volunteer for the French fondue field trip, and watch him break his personal record in the fifty-meter dash at track meets.

Our fears are rarely true, yet they feel true and can hold us back from abundance.

So let's dissolve any of yours that may have come up since you began monetizing your mission.

Do you fear that more money/bigger business, will mean you lose your free time? That you'll have to work eighty hours a week? That you'll burn out? Do you fear you won't have any privacy if you're more visible and well-known? Do you fear more money will make you selfish or greedy?

In addition to the release strategies I shared earlier, you can find several people who are doing what you want to do, earning the money you'd like to receive, and find out how they've set up their lives in a way that disproves your fear.

If you're afraid you'll have to work long hours to make a million dollars a year, find an entrepreneur making seven figures who only works four days a week or takes the last week of each month off or takes the entire month of August and December off every year. I know multiple friends and colleagues who fit this description.

• • •

In the documentary film, *Supersize Me*, the host commits to eating McDonald's every day for thirty days in a row. By the self-established rules of his experiment, he had to say "yes" anytime he was asked if he wanted to "supersize" his order. It's a wild film that always fills me with gratitude for the superfoods and health practices I choose every day. However, in the right context, the SUPERSIZE ME practice can yield great things.

What I will share next are some strategies that have SUPERSIZED the results of the Abundance Accelerator. Review the following list and see if you're up for supersizing your abundance by putting these into practice for the next thirty days.

Abundance Tracking

There's a saying in metaphysics: what gets tracked increases. During the Abundance Accelerator, try tracking every action you take toward your abundance goals as well as all abundance received. To supersize this technique, also track signs/affirmations and your mindset practices (such as meditation or reading this section of the book). Imagine your tracker is a game board to give your brain a message that abundance is FUN and prove that you are making progress regardless of immediate results. We're invoking the principle of focus on ACTION vs OUTCOME, a practice that has helped me stay motivated when manifestation takes longer than I'd like while simultaneously, because of the subconscious programming tracking facilitates, accelerates success.

You can create your own tracking file or use the Abundance Accelerator Workbook:

On your tracking sheet:

1. Goal: Write your abundance goal for the next month.
2. Mindset: What activity/practice you do each day to support your belief in and alignment with that goal.
3. Outreach: Each action you take to reach out to a prospective client/customer or referral resource/partner.
4. Conversations: Each conversation/meeting you have with a prospective client/customer or referral resource/partner.
5. Negative responses: The action here will be to ask anyone who decides not to say yes now if they will share why and what would have made it a yes for them. This will reveal any adjustments you want to consider in investment rate, offer, benefit explanations, or bonus.

6. Positive responses: YESs! With exact $$$$$$ amount. You can set up this game board however you like—handwritten with hearts, digital, or a simple spreadsheet or chart.

Example:
In the next month, I am so grateful to receive $100K.

ACTION	DESCRIPTION	FIELD NOTES
Mindset	6/23: Six-phase meditation on YouTube, tapping, self-hypnosis	Felt positive and excited
Outreach	6/23: Sent video emails to three people on Heart list, sent pitches to three people for guest speaking engagements, and reached out to five people on LinkedIn who commented on video about publishing.	
Conversations/ Offers made	6/23: Zoomed with three prospective clients	
YESs	6/23: Two signed up for group program at $10K each	
Nos	6/23: One person decided she did not have the resources to invest at this time. Said she would have done it now if $3K instead of $10K. She asked to be on email list and said she has a goal to start in the fall. Gave her free ticket to next event. Made a date to talk Sept 1.	
$ Earned	$20K	

ACTION	DESCRIPTION	FIELD NOTES
OR YOU CAN TRACK THE WHOLE MONTH WITH an I for every action taken in each category.		
Mindset	III	
Outreach	IIIIIIIIIIIIIIIIIIIIIIIII IIII	
Conversations with offer	IIIIIIIIIIIIIIIIII	
Nos	II	
Yess/ $ earned	IIII	

The final component of the Abundance Accelerator: *Rewarding Action!*

Make a list of ten things you love. Try pleasure bundling—giving yourself one of these treats every time you take the action you committed to that day. By rewarding action vs result, we make the action itself exciting, detach from outcome, and reprogram our brains for success.

If you hit inner resistance or inner challenges, go to the release techniques in the previous chapter and clear each day for five to ten minutes.

If you want to join our next Abundance Accelerator and take these steps with our community, go here:

Story Time

Jen was one of our first clients to use the Accelerator. She is a full-time single mom who lost both parents in a short period of time right before the pandemic hit. Although she'd had a successful, thriving business as a coach and consultant for almost twenty years, Jen found herself stuck around finances in the midst of her grief and being overwhelmed by home school and the heartbreak of racial injustices pummeling America and her own community.

"I don't know what to do to start generating business again," she said.

We brought a group of Thought Leader Academy members to try out the process that had worked for me every time I became stuck. Jen took the steps outlined in this chapter. Here's what happened, in Jen's own words:

"In the summer, Q3, I started to get stressed out about not having enough clients and money flow coming in. I was in a doubt/lack mindset; what was I going to do?

I did Sara's Abundance Accelerator training, and it totally shifted everything!

- I wrote and published two books last year.
- I began intentionally contacting people and companies daily and weekly.
- I did all the challenges from Sara and the calls inspired and fueled me!
- I tracked all my contacts on a spreadsheet and continued to follow up with people, and past clients started contacting me again for my business. It was like magic!
- We created an abundance pod within Thought Leader Academy for accountability, successes, and support to stay in Abundance mindset.
- By the time fall hit in Q4, I had sold $100K in consulting projects and coaching programs (and had proposals out for another 230k).
- This completely made up for the slow business in the rest of the year. I trusted myself again and know now I can manifest money if I get intentional, track my progress, and have a circle of support!

SUPERSIZE YOU?

In addition to tracking action, signs, and results, another supersize move is to think about your community. Jim Rohn is famous for saying, "Your life will reflect the five people with whom you spend the most time." He mentored Tony Robbins, who went on to demonstrate that the five people or groups with whom we spend the most time will determine your level of health, success, leadership, and yes, money.

Over the past ten years, building up from $20K to $2 million+/year, I've seen physical proof that:

YOUR NETWORK IS YOUR NET WORTH.

Last year, I heard that if you put a baby shark in a small tank, the shark will grow to about eight inches long. You put the same shark in the ocean, it will grow to ten-fifteen feet. When we Be + (Release) + Do alone, we will get results. One our own, we may grow eight inches. But if we want to grow ten feet, we jump into the ocean and let the community of vibrating life and the vastness of our container stretch us our full, giant, genius, powerful potential. Jen and Gina and Donna and Diane and Patty and all the mothers, coaches, experts, activists, entrepreneurs, writers, and Thought Leaders who have participated in the Abundance Accelerator experienced growth from doing the actions *together.*

This fourth and final strategy—community—is an abundance producer of itself and is also an amplifier of all the other strategies you choose to use.

The summer I first decided to change my financial destiny and drove around every day listening to Tony Robbins on YouTube. Tony mentioned the five people concept so many times, it finally landed in my heart. I remember him also saying that before Michael Jordan became the best basketball player in the world, he always sought out players who were seven times better than he was. Tony began to research other people who'd reached the level of "best" in their fields of play and found that they too sought out as many opportunities as possible to play, train, study, compete with people better than they were. Tennis players, oboe prodigies, chess players, surgeons—the takeaway is that being with people ahead of us in knowledge, skill, and performance will exponentially improve our game. Tony and others found this was true about wealth as well. Many experts have demonstrated that our *wealth and success will reflect the five people or groups with whom we spend the most time.*

When I was a writer-coach making $20,000 a year, most of my friends were amazing, creative individuals who also struggled with money. I'd heard of women who made six, multiple six, or seven figures a year, but I wasn't connected with them; I wasn't in community with them.

Increasing our wealth doesn't mean we ditch people who don't share that goal or haven't achieved it. It may mean, though, that we will benefit greatly from adding connections and communities of others who have created the kind of financial abundance we desire.

Why?

If we continue thinking, feeling, and behaving the way we have until now, we will not expand, increase, and grow. Being only around people who think, feel, behave, and act as we do at our current abundance level will keep us right where we are. While we can absolutely read about, listen to, and imagine people who've achieved the financial and impact goals we desire, the fast track is to "get in the room where it happens."

Give yourself the gift and the stretch of valuing yourself enough to join a community and build relationships with people who have achieved or even vastly exceeded your goal. Very quickly, with little effort, you will hear how they think, see what they do, watch how they lead, and overcome their own resistance and be able to adopt the same solutions, strategies, and techniques they use to create wealth in your own life.

That summer driving around in my car, I'd listened to Tony Robbins enough to be convinced that I needed to "be in the room" with women who were earning six figures plus, but where were those women? Within two weeks of my declaration to find people seven steps ahead of me in earning, I received an email to attend an online workshop. I signed up for $200, liked the facilitators, and was inspired by their service-centered approach to business and their story of financial empowerment through making a positive impact on the world.

I took one of their lists of ten recommended action steps. That's all I could will myself to do since I didn't have the RELEASE steps I would discover later to clear procrastination and resistance. I made an extra $1,000 that week. I knew one strategy was not going to get me to six figures, and I was beginning to comprehend that trying to do all this work on my own was not a stellar plan. But the cost of joining the community run by these two amazing women was $10,000. I had never invested more than a few hundred dollars in myself. My brain screamed that to make such a commitment would be impulsive, reckless, dangerous. I also understood now that nothing in my life was going to change if I kept doing what I was doing and being around the same people I was around, so I joined.

Suddenly I was living in a magical world of women as committed to financial freedom as to serving the world. I'd burned my one remaining boat and had to change. As people in Alcoholics Anonymous say when they first enter the program, "We were as desperate as a drowning woman (they say man) seizing a life preserver." That was me in my first prosperous, abundant community. I vowed to do whatever the business coaching program curriculum suggested. In eleven weeks, I'd made back the entire investment for the program. By month three, I'd earned more than I'd earned the previous two years combined.

I learned the core issue for me wasn't the money; it was about valuing myself and the work. It was about taking the risk to be visible and to be rejected. It was about friendships and partnerships and collaboration. It turned out that Abundance, Richness, and Wealth is a team sport.

I met Rachel, who made over $100,000 a year as a psychotherapist and would go on to sign an annual $350,000 contract with a corporation she loves, working part-time. I'd meet Lisa, a mission-driven lawyer who focused on supporting female entrepreneurs. Lisa crossed the $600,000 mark the year I met her, and as far as I know, has now entered multiple-seven figures/year. Women from twenty different countries, women for whom English was a second or third language, and yet they felt called to serve English-speaking audiences with their gifts and who fought through the beliefs they'd be overlooked or passed over because of it. Women who had PhDs and women who never finished high school, women in their twenties and women in their seventies, women who walked, and women in wheelchairs and on crutches. We were in it together, and they showed me that not a single one of my excuses held any weight. The only reason I wasn't creating wealth was because of my limited mindset and actions, and no one there was going to stand for me reaching anything less than my full potential.

I've since participated in almost a dozen different business, entrepreneur, writing, artistic, and financial communities. I currently work with two mentors and am members of both their communities. One of my mentors lives in Paris, is an incredible mother and partner, works only one hour a day most days, and brings in $3-5M/year. She serves with courage, soul, and the absolute belief you can create major abundance and have your life back.

My other mentor is a fiery, passionate leader who makes over $20M/year. Yes, that's $20 million. For sure she's seven steps ahead of me.

I joined my mentor's elite mastermind of multi-seven-figure, mission-driven entrepreneurs way before I felt ready to be there, way before I hit that million mark. I thought of Michael Jordan—before he was Michael Jordan to the world—looking for a game of pick-up with people seven times better than he was. I humbly showed up, knowing I had much to learn and that, although I was still working towards greater levels of impact and income, I could start serving, giving, and supporting every member of that group from the moment I joined. I can thank these communities I've had the privilege to be part of not only for my continued revenue expansion but also for my four closest friends in the world. You'll meet some of these women in the coming pages.

Do you have a rich, abundant, prosperous destiny stretching community in place? Thanks to our virtual world, it has never been easier to find a group for anything you desire.

You can join masterminds, coaching groups, referral groups, classes, networking organizations, mentorship programs, take online classes, masterclasses, and workshops with leaders who will teach you their strategies and master practices.

By being "in the room where it happens," you'll find yourself in partnership with people you admire, with people who are doing exactly what you hope to do. Your five-year plan will become your one-year plan.

Creating this type of community for our clients was my top priority when we opened Thought Leader Academy. I loved coaching clients one-on-one, but if I continued only offering individual coaching, they'd never have to shift and stretch to the extent possible if we came together in a group. I'd been forever changed for the good, thanks to the communities others had generously extended to me, and I vowed to do anything I could to pay this gift forward. I see the magic taking place every week. Joint ventures, collaborative book launches, grants generated for those who don't yet have the investment resources. Members who thought writing a book or making six figures was a pipe dream smashing that goal and setting a new one. Together we get to be the rising tide that raises all ships.

Like me, you may not feel ready or maybe even worthy to be "in the room" with some of these groups at the start. But enter anyway. Go in before you're ready. Before you have anything figured out. Before you even understand what everyone is talking about (that was me in every group I joined for at least the first six months). After stretching and releasing all your gremlins, you'll find that you were always worthy and capable and wanted and loved enough to be there, that you are a gift to that room, even on day one. You'll find it was the room of your destiny all along.

CHAPTER NINE

Lead

CONGRATULATIONS!!! WOOO-HOOOO!! You've taken the Shero's journey through all five strategies of the Thought Leader Path.

You're Awesome!

You're Amazing!

I am SOOO excited to see you put these strategies into action and blow our minds-blow the mind of the world!

I also know that some days feel exhilarating and some days feel like we're Sisyphus, pushing a giant boulder up a mountain. When I have a Sisyphus day, something that lifts me the most is hearing stories of people who've faced similar challenges, broken through, and ascended to love, joy, abundance, and success.

By reading this book and beginning to implement the Thought Leader strategies, you are part of a collective, a movement of kick-ass leaders who are changing the world. To give some continued motivation and inspiration, I'm going to share the personal stories of some amazing Thought Leader Academy members who are doing this work, using the five strategies, every day. I wanted you to hear directly from these leaders-some who started Thought Leader Academy on the day it began, and some who just started their journey a few months ago. They volunteered to share in their own words, with no filter or narration from me, who they are, where they started, and what they're creating now. I hope as you read, your vision will be affirmed, expanded, and fired with new passion. YOU ARE ONE with anything you desire to create, and we are all here cheering you on already. As I said at the start of this book, you are part of this community, our Thought Leader family now.

I can't wait to continue the journey with you. We want to meet you, know you, and continue to support you at every step. Now that you've read the book, you can connect with us right now, here:

https://form.jotform.com/SaraConnellCoaching/TLA-Catalyst

We are SOOOO EXCITED for yours to be the next SUCCESS story we blast out to the world.

IT IS DONE!

Love,

Sara

CHAPTER TEN
TLA Stories

Stefani Fryzel

I'm Stefani Fryzel (aka DYLN). I'm an artist/songwriter and author of *Self-Care for the Creative: A Survival Guide for Creatives, Empaths and Highly Sensitive People*, and creator of The Songwriter Series, an online mentoring platform for artists and songwriters. I also host the *Self-Care for the Creative* podcast where I discuss self-care strategies for people in creative communities. My mission is to help creative empaths thrive through community, self-discovery, and self-care.

When I first started TLA, I had the idea for my book and no idea what to do next. The only thing I had done was a book proposal (which I didn't even end up using in the end). Being in the music industry, I knew next to no one in the writer or author world, and I didn't even know where or how to start. I knew I had a big idea with a big mission behind it and all these business ideas. I was at the point in my career where I knew it was time to start investing in coaching.

The biggest mind shift for me in TLA has been expanding my ability to BELIEVE IN MYSELF. Being amongst a community of mostly women and surrounding yourself with the people who are brave enough to go for the goals, feel the fear, and do it anyway is totally contagious. Powerful things happen when you're immersed with people who are all yessing their dreams in some way. Sometimes we need to see examples of other women doing the things we want to do so that we can believe we can do it too. That's what TLA is. An energetic upgrade.

The thing I'm most proud of is BECOMING AN AUTHOR and launching a completely new career and business for myself where I get to take my passions and multiply them with purpose.

What's next is serving as many creatives as possible, empowering them with tools, techniques, and encouraging them to share their voices! I know how hard it can be to struggle with mental illness and endure the artist's journey. My goal is to make that path a little bit easier for all artists out there who have something important to say!

You can find out more at www.stefanifryzel.com.

Lorry Leigh Belhumeur

I'm Lorry Leigh Belhumeur, PhD. I am now also the bestselling, award-winning author of the book *Mastering Resilience*. After thirty years working in mental health and well-being, my friends and colleagues started calling me Dr. Resilience and I'm now known as America's Super-resilient expert. My mission is to help people transform all kinds of adversity into a purposeful, joyful, and fulfilled life.

Before joining Thought Leader Academy, I knew I had a book in me. I've been in clinical practice for thirty years, and for at least seven years before I joined, I was attempting to write. I know I'm a disciplined person, I got a PhD for goodness sake, I run a nonprofit organization that's had exponential growth well into eight figures, and yet, the book remained a daydream, not a reality.

When I joined TLA, I discovered a loving level of accountability and experienced the benefits of being in a community of other authors, experts, and leaders. I looked forward to the weekly TLA sessions and learned that what I was feeling, the challenges, and the progress I faced in writing the book were normal.

I got to look up the ladder and watch my peers in TLA publishing bestselling books, and it made me know it was possible. I saw that the business of their lives did not keep them from publishing their books. (Other women were running businesses, one had six kids, others wrote through health challenges.) I shifted to a "no excuses here!" mentality. Those sessions were not only motivating, but inspiring.

All this prompted MASSIVE ACTION and I finished my first book, and at the time of writing this, I have two more in process.

The best parts:

The book hit bestseller on day one and has remained in the top ten for three months (through the writing of this today).

In the last thirty days, the book has sold over 250 copies at Barnes & Noble this month, and the number of five-star reviews blows my mind.

The book has received accolades from groups that were not even my target audiences such as young adults and attorneys, which demonstrated impact beyond what I'd even imagined.

I get to do international book signings and I've just been invited to speak at a huge expo conference where I'll be paid five figures to present from the stage and the book was chosen to be included in a celebrity gift box.

This has all led to a big uplevel of my brand and given me the opportunity to launch a course to go with the book, and opportunities to speak and joint venture with other leaders. I even transformed my wardrobe, trading bland, neutral colors for vibrant fabrics, power suits, and unique and joyful clothing that expresses my authentic style.

Something I never expected was that when I released the book, I also released weight. I didn't change anything or try. I'd done a tremendous amount of inner work, and yet another level and the more mindset work I did and courageous action I took, the more transformation took place.

What I'm most excited about next is to bring our Super-resilient Leadership to businesses, organizations, communities so we can improve the mental wellness of every employee and leader.

You can check out my work on resilience at: www.superresilient.com.

Amy S. Peele

I am a bestselling and award-winning author, sought after speaker, and the creator of Laughter-Stretch-Breath, LSB, more on that later. For the record, I didn't start out knowing or believing I could do any of these things; matter-of-fact, if you had asked me ten years ago if I would BE any of these things, I would recommend you see a therapist and start medications.

My journey with Sara Connell started over almost thirty years ago when Sara became my life coach, and it was one of the most important decisions I ever made. I joined TLA because I already knew that if I could dream it, I could make it happen with Sara's support, guidance, and coaching.

I wrote and self-published a memoir, *Aunt Mary's Guide to Raising Children the Old-Fashioned Way*, in 2009. I was working full-time as director of clinical operations for one of the biggest organ transplant programs in the world–UCSF. We performed over six hundred transplants annually–a true, park-yourself-at-the-door job. AND I wanted to write a memoir for an upcoming family reunion and had convinced myself that was impossible. With Sara's coaching and a basket of tips she shared, it happened, and I even went on a book tour with my mom introducing me. What a healing journey it was for both of us and folks really enjoyed it. In 2023, I signed with MUSE Literary, who I learned about through TLA, to write the second edition of the memoir and narrate the audio this year.

As I was getting ready to retire in 2014, I decided I would write a mystery series where I would kill the people I didn't like at work and use their organs for transplant–why waste the kill! Fast forward, I'm now the author of a bestselling and award-winning mystery trilogy, *CUT–MATCH–HOLD*, published by She Writes Press. All three books are also available on audio. For the record, I'm not an English major; matter-of-fact, I wasn't the best speller so I had assumed that I couldn't write a story, not to mention a book. I have learned through TLA and Sara's coaching that my doubts, aka gremlins, didn't get to decide what I could and couldn't do. I've learned over the years to acknowledge them and then continue to set about achieving my dreams. I can tell with 100 percent certainty, if I had not had Sara on my side and the TLA community cheering me on, I would not have achieved my writing and publishing goals.

I also continued to follow my dreams; I became a certified hatha yoga teacher at the Chopra Center in 2016 and was trained to lead Laughter Yoga at UCSF in 2018. Witnessing the state of our world during and after Covid, I wanted to offer some coaching to the educators in our county. I reached out to MaryJane Burke, the superintendent of Marin

County schools, and offered to come teach some simple breathing techniques that would encourage educators to take deep breaths as well as do some stretching right in their chairs. I added a dollop of laughter at the end, and voilà, LSB was born. THEY LOVED IT!!! And while I offered to do it pro bono, they declined and paid me through their wellness budget. LSB has taken off like wildfire. Educators can't wait to come to my class, leaving their phones and emails behind for thirty minutes, then returning to their desks, refreshed and centered, ready to complete their workday. I am also teaching at a local retirement home, and it brings me such joy to teach, and they seem to love it as well. I deliberately don't use the word yoga in the description as that word sometimes conjures up pretzel people or an assortment of headstands and handstands. We can all learn to use our mind-body-spirit, move into our bodies, take deep belly breaths, stretch every part of our body, and have a laugh, which produces endorphins.

I'm excited for what's next for me as I write a stand-alone romcom for my literary agent who signed me after I wrote and published my first mystery, *CUT*. Not in a million years would I have thought I could ever get a literary agent.

I've met some lifelong friends through TLA, and I am forever grateful that I had the courage to declare my dreams and have Sara Connell be there to inspire me, witness them, and guide me along my path. You can find me and learn all about my journey, books, and LSB by going to my website www.amyspeele.com.

BE WELL and REMEMBER TO TAKE DEEP BREATHS AND LAUGH OFTEN.

Chris Williams

I had been a stay-at-home mom to my three boys for seventeen years when I went through a divorce and started a new life.

I was determined to be happy and staying in a toxic relationship where my ex-husband was content to just survive was not in alignment for me anymore. I was struggling mentally, emotionally, and then the big red flag of physical illness hit. This was the sign that it was no longer okay to stay. I was dying inside, my self-esteem was crumbling, and I received a sign loud and clear that it was time. I ended up in the hospital for three days with severe stomach pains. I could barely stand up and lying down didn't help either. They did blood tests every four hours and a colonoscopy to try and figure out what was wrong. But every test came back normal. So after three days in the hospital all by myself (no visits from the hubby), I came home. I was so tired and remember lying on the couch when my ex asked me if I would be making dinner or just lying on the couch. WOW.

The next week I went to see my doctor, and she looked at me and said, "I don't know what is going on, but you either need to change the way you are looking at whatever is happening, or leave the situation." For some reason, that was the permission I needed to hear. So I decided it was time to start living an empowered life and create something amazing where I would not only be able to support myself and my children, but THRIVE and be happy. I wanted to build something where I would feel purposeful, impactful, fulfilled, and create the financial independence I desired so I could create a life of more choices. I wanted to still be a present mom, be available for my boys, and be celebrated for my independence, vision, and creativity, and not squashed. And so I hopped onto the mantra, "She believed she could and she did."

With $25 in my pocket and an agreement for some child support and alimony, I left the fifty acres, my farm house, my gardens, and I asked myself what I wanted to do. I had been naturally drawn to health and wellness my entire life. From baking and cooking from scratch, growing veggies organically on our farm, to teaching others how to make bread and live more holistically, that had been a calling on my heart. I remember a friend told me once that I should start a blog on what I do on the farm, as she would love to read it. I had no idea at the time that I could actually make a living teaching holistic health practices.

I followed the nudges of my heart and decided that in order to have the freedom financially and time wise, it would be best to be my own boss. A business that would be helping others and following my heart for natural health. So I went to school to become a massage therapist. I already had my yoga teacher certification and had been teaching two classes a week part-time for years while I raised my kids, so the idea of blending multiple modalities to create my own business felt exciting.

After I graduated from massage school, I found space in a wellness center to rent a room, but I had no idea how to run a business, find clients, or even keep my books. That's the problem when you learn a modality or get a wellness certification. You learn how to perform a skill or help others, but you're missing the business side of things. The same thing happened when I went to school to add a certification in functional nutritional therapy. Great skills to help others, zero skills in building a business. And again, when I added prenatal massage certification and transformational health and life coaching certifications to my portfolio and service offerings. Fabulous training in the modality to serve others, but still, no guidance on how to build a business.

I was in my late forties and I didn't have time to waste. So while the first few years I tried to piece things together and asked a few massage therapists what they were doing, I was still barely making ends meet. I had spent tens of thousands of dollars on certifications, and it was time to make that back and get out of the $20,000 debt I was in paying for my education. My credit cards were maxed out, I had no savings, and found myself determined to figure it out. I knew if I wanted to create real income doing what I loved, I needed to learn what I didn't know from an expert. I also saw my colleagues barely making it too. It seemed crazy to me that we weren't taught how to set up a business, learning the basics of sales and marketing to actually help us succeed. So I hired help. I reached out to someone who I saw succeeding and teaching a heart-centered method of growing her coaching business in a way that felt exciting and in alignment with my values as a wellness practitioner. And with guidance, my business began to soar.

I began implementing what I learned, and within six months, I had crossed the six-figure mark in my business. In one year, I had created multiple six figures, and in three years, I crossed the $1 million mark. Others began reaching out to me, asking me what I was doing. And with generosity and joy, I happily shared what I was doing to create income and success. As more women wellness entrepreneurs began reaching out to me, it became clear that my role was to help other women set up their business for success too. It was a natural and organic shifting that was happening. I had no intention of being a business coach. I was just sharing what I knew worked for me in a way that felt good and saw others using my teachings and getting results too.

I decided to put what I did into a system and process that others could follow. So that they could collapse the timeline to their success and not struggle like I did in the beginning. I wanted more women to have the practical how-tos to take their love for helping others and monetize their certifications so they could be well paid while sharing their gifts with others. And without trading their well-being or integrity for success. There were lots of ways being taught in the coaching world to build a business, but not many that worked well for heart-centered women entrepreneurs. Most were based on the masculine marketing and sales tactics of booking a free call to sign a client. And that just never felt right to me. While I have no problem supporting people on a call at the right time, trying to sell my program to a complete stranger the first time we had a conversation felt heavy. I felt pressured to "close the deal." I was told I needed to "overcome their objections" on the call. This method felt salesy and inauthentic to who I was. So I stopped booking free discovery sessions, and instead, I began nurturing relationships.

I realized that what was missing was a critical component that was based on the feminine aspect of nurturing. I created The Nurture Method® based on three simple business basics that get results.

Putting these three business basics into action allowed me to cross the $1 million mark in my business in just three years. And I've gone on to support hundreds of more women to build a financially profitable and sustainable six-figure plus business they love inside my year-long program Activate Abundance Academy®. Without the cringey sales tactics, fear-based marketing, or hustling to get clients.

It's a proven process that works so well, one of my clients went from bankrupt to six figures in one year. Others have paid off their debts, contributed to their family with their business profits, put kids through college, paid for travel, and are consistently attracting clients they love to work with. They feel fulfilled, supported, confident, and finally have the knowledge and community to help them succeed.

The beauty of all this is that when they succeed, it means they are helping others live happier, healthier lives, and transforming our world for the better. And that creates ripple effects that transcend what we can see. Happier, healthier people, families, relationships, businesses make our world go round.

We need more empowered women being well paid helping people. It's my mission to show other women coaches and wellness professionals how they can do it too. I'll share my free checklist to help you too. You can get the Six-Figure Business Basics Checklist here: https://chriswilliams.kartra.com/page/BizBasics.

If you have it in your heart to grow your coaching or wellness business, you can totally do it. I believe in you. I know you can do it because I have. From struggling to make ends meet as a single mom, to traveling the world with my family, and having a business that helps others is my dream come true. Just this week, I completed a three-week trip in Europe to see the lavender fields in France, a bucket list item I've wanted to do for thirty years. I hiked the Alps with my (new) husband, took my three boys to Paris and the Pyrenees mountains in Catalonia, and all of this is possible because of the courage to follow the whispering of my heart.

Feel free to join me inside my free Facebook community (https://www.facebook.com/groups/abundantempoweredfeminineleaders) where I teach live weekly soulful business trainings each Monday at 4:00 p.m. EST. I'd love to meet you and hear your vision. Come say hello. I'm cheering you on.

To your ultimate abundance,
Chris

Molly McGrath

As a lifelong deep thinker and feeler, I have always been driven by a thirst for knowledge. It was in 1997 that I first discovered the world of "coaching," and from that moment on, I was captivated. This newfound passion became the driving force behind my personal and professional growth, and in 2008, I took the leap to establish my own business as a legal coach, consultant, and recruiter.

From the very beginning, my vision has been to revolutionize the employer-employee experience, shifting it from a mere transactional interaction to a deep, meaningful relationship. Through my dedication and commitment, I have authored three books on this subject, regularly sharing my insights through my weekly blogs and podcast episodes.

It was during one of my podcast interviews in the spring of 2020 that I had a transformative conversation with a fellow coach who had recently released a book. Intrigued by her writing process, she introduced me to TLA, and my curiosity was piqued. Following that encounter, I interviewed Sara, on my podcast in December 2020. Little did I know that this meeting would lead me down an unexpected path—I found myself becoming a part of TLA.

At that time, I had no intention of embarking on another book-writing journey. Having undergone the arduous and costly process three times before, I believed my authorship days were behind me. However, during a call with Sara that lasted just fourteen minutes, she keenly recognized the essence of my mission and movement and presented me with a title for my next book—one she insisted the world needed to read. I couldn't deny that this message had to be shared with the world.

My mission, my movement, revolves around reshaping workplace energy and redefining the ambiguous term that business owners often throw around—culture. I am determined to transform the widespread employee resignation into a process of restoration, fostering an environment where employees feel seen, heard, valued, and empowered. A place where they can go from floundering to flourishing.

Since the late nineties, I have built five national organizations. Through staffing, coaching, consulting, and directing presidents and founders, I have worked with over four thousand law firms. My expertise lies in executive-level leadership, continuous improvement, and empowering teams to enter new markets, harnessing the power of partner ecosystems to drive profitability. As one of the top 10 percent of global podcasters, and having maintained a consistent blogging schedule since 2008, I appeared successful on paper. Yet, my inner critic constantly whispered doubts—I wasn't working hard enough, doing enough, or possessing the qualities of a "real" million-dollar business owner. This self-sabotaging loop hindered the development of my million-dollar mindset, anchored deep within my soul. That was until I joined TLA.

However, my greatest achievement since becoming a part of TLA surpasses publishing my third number one Amazon bestselling book, which I am undeniably proud of. It even surpasses getting through the Ted Talk process and submitting my application in summer of 2023. It surpasses the clarity I gained in setting my pricing and raising my fees, which was a remarkable feat. What I'm most proud of is the transformation of my mindset. The mantra at TLA is, "I can and I will—watch me." I take immense pride in my mindset and my ability to silence my inner demons, shifting towards an abundance mindset. I now listen to and trust my intuition, equipped with the tools to dismantle the self-defeating stories I once believed. I understand when to refine and scale back, recognizing the signs of exertion and exhaustion. Equally important, I know when to fully commit and scale forward, driven by the joy of accomplishment rather than a sense of obligation. I can distinguish between these two voices and acknowledge the one that truly matters.

During the past two years as a member of TLA, I embarked on a profound journey of self-discovery. For the first time in my life, I have defined what success really means to me, on my own terms. I am just emerging from this transformative experience, forever changed.

To witness the incredible works that have emerged from TLA, I invite you to visit my book portal www.fixmybossbook.com. There, you will find my latest book and the book portal that TLA gave me the power to ignite change and reshape the way we perceive work and leadership.

Audrey Faust

Just like every January past, as 2023 began, I found myself nestled in my favorite chair, dreaming, and setting the goals that would shape the coming year. This time, though, the intention I set was particularly ambitious: "This year," I wrote in my journal, "I'm going to write a book." The thought wasn't new, but the commitment was. It felt like a silent pact between myself and the many women I've coached and mentored, the commitment of a journey that promised to light their path to prosperity by revealing the tremendous power within themselves to build wealth.

In my journey as a coach, I'd come across countless women who echoed the same sentiment when it came to saving, "There's simply nothing left." This was an equation I knew I could rebalance. I began to teach them to regard savings not as an option but as an obligation, a "self-love" bill if you will, just as nonnegotiable as an electric bill.

Before joining me, many women would speak with their accountants or banks without truly understanding their own financial standing. This often led to unpleasant surprises, like owing a hefty tax bill or not getting approved for financing. But as we created a path together, they started to reclaim control over their numbers. They found the strength to look their business in the eye and understand its strengths and weaknesses. Their ignorance became empowerment, and their businesses flourished in response. They became empowered to make educated financial decisions and take their business to the next level.

There was one woman, a shining example of grit, who had built a seven-figure empire. Yet her financial standing didn't mirror her success. Her deep-seated beliefs from childhood had always placed her last in line, often prioritizing her business and employees over her own needs. Despite her business success, she was left with nothing, even falling into debt. Witnessing this broke my heart.

That's when I knew my mission had to expand. My financial acumen and coaching skills needed to reach every woman who had ever felt unable to build a secure financial future for themselves and their families. I decided to write my experiences, my teachings, my journey from a net worth of zero to a multi seven-figure standing over two decades. But here was the catch—I was a CFO and a financial coach, not a writer. What did I know about writing?

Enter Sara. I found her through a group session organized by my business coach. The universe truly does have a sense of humor, because unbeknownst to me, one of the coaches in that session was a book-writing coach. I felt an instant connection with Sara and quickly jumped into her free events. After attending her two-day intensive writing workshop, I knew she was the person to guide me on my writing journey.

Financing the coaching wasn't initially in my plans. But after experiencing her techniques firsthand, I knew her insights were worth every penny. It wasn't until her retreat in New Orleans that year that I officially joined her group, Thought Leader Academy. The retreat, with its focus on mindset and motivation rather than writing, was transformative and one of the best I had ever attended. As Bob Proctor says, "Success is 95 percent mindset and only 5 percent strategy," and I experienced this truth firsthand.

A few months into Sara's program, I've already seen a massive shift in everything I do. My book, which was merely an outline before, is now 95 percent complete. I've connected with Mary, my exceptional writing coach and editor, whose kindness and support are unparalleled. Sara's unique ideas and solutions during our group coaching sessions have been instrumental in propelling my business forward. One such nugget was the creation of a five-question application form for potential clients, helping me streamline calls and focus on impactful conversations.

Just two months in with Sara and the TLA group, and I'm already fueled with anticipation and inspiration. Sara and her team of expert writing coaches guide us as we uncover new opportunities, helping us translate our unique stories into words. Being part of this collective, all striving to express our individual genius, is inspiring. I'm eagerly looking forward to what lies ahead.

To every woman reading this, let me impart a message from my heart to yours: you deserve a place at the financial table. Never allow anyone, especially not yourself, to undermine that. Understanding your numbers, the ebbs and flows of your finances, and building a secure future is not just a far-off dream; it's entirely possible. More than that, it's your inherent right, and indeed your responsibility, to claim that knowledge and empowerment for you and the next generation of young women following your path.

You owe it to yourself to master the language of wealth and navigate your own path to financial prosperity. This journey needn't be complex; it's an open road and you're in the driver's seat. And to assist you, I've designed three free calculators that simplify the process of wealth creation, breaking down the exact steps you need to build your wealth and achieve financial independence. Embrace this journey with my tools in hand, and remember, you're not just a passenger but the driver of your financial destiny. So, get ready to accelerate towards prosperity—your link to financial empowerment is just a click away: https://www.audreyfaustconsulting.com/wealth-building-bundle-access.

Audrey Faust, MBA – CFO and Financial Coach
www.audrefaustconsulting.com

Rosalyn Rourke

I never dreamed of becoming a writer. I was in attendance at a TEDx group coaching in 2021 when Sara Connell appeared as an invited guest speaker because the group had expressed interest in book writing. At the end of her dynamic talk, Sara asked the group how many of us had already written or wished to write a book. Every hand went up, except mine. Sara offered a free week of book coaching at an upcoming event she was holding. Since I could attend virtually, I felt a push to clear my calendar and attend. But, on the first day, my attitude was lacking. I showed up late, wondering why I was even in the room, since I had no interest in writing a book.

And then something happened. I was mesmerized by Sara's ability to make every person know their story was worth telling. And I did have a story.

Three years earlier, my precious thirty-nine-year-old younger daughter, Melissa, unexpectedly died. When the police said rigor mortis had already set in, so she could not be revived, I was sure my life was over. And it was for a while. This was the nightmare that kept on going. I'm not sure which stage was worse: the shock of disbelief or the pain of knowing Melissa was forever gone from our daily lives.

But for me, she wasn't gone. I felt a close connection to her and as time passed, I felt I needed to be her voice in the world. When Melissa died, I was happily retired at age seventy, and Melissa and I had finally arrived at an amazing rapprochement after years of struggle around her body size and weight. As a psychotherapist for over thirty years, I was aware that I was repeating patterns of three-plus generations of mothers and daughters with judgment and pain about body issues. Melissa and I had both done a lot of psychological and spiritual work to heal the pain of our rift, but it wasn't until I was gifted a session with Ireland's most famous mystic, Lorna Byrne, that everything changed. Though Melissa was not present, Lorna spoke almost entirely about her, helping me to focus on my worry as poisonous to Melissa and our relationship. After the session, my judgment toward my daughter miraculously ceased. Weeks later, Melissa began a deeper connection with intuition. She received messages that were eerily specific like, "You will not have a need for money, so work for free." She was transformed by the messages and began to have an inner authority when she spoke from intuition. On her last day on Earth she wrote, "Mom, share with your full brilliance, no matter what!"

I thought my sharing with the world was to be a TEDx talk. But after meeting Sara, joining Thought Leader Academy, and meeting the perfect editor, Mary Nelligan, my book was born: *When Wisdom Arrives: From Imagined Unworthiness to Freedom*. The book is a mix of fable and memoir. The fable introduces eleven-year-old Gem, who feels unworthy and unlovable because of her body size. A character named Wisdom demonstrates to Gem that her feelings of unworthiness are imagined and her looping thoughts and feelings are keeping her stuck. Through games and loving conversations, Wisdom teaches Gem that profound okayness is available in the NOW of every moment despite outer circumstances. The memoir companion details my own experience of reclaiming okayness. When I stopped feeding past and future looping thoughts and feelings around Melissa's death, my intense grief and struggle were released in the NOW.

When the book was complete, I thought I would be done with what life was asking of me. But as I participated in TLA and collaborated with other mission driven, soulful thought leaders, my mission got clearer. I saw there is a real movement available for us to join together in standing-up for each other's worth.

I am now an author, master enneagram teacher, and oneness coach, as well as a coach to coaches and retired people who are looking to make an impact in the world and find inner peace in the NOW. My mission is to help every interested person discover that their sense of unworthiness is imagined. Why does it matter what people believe? A false belief in unworthiness eats away at our sense of belonging, connection, and self-care. A belief in unworthiness is like slow torture and a kind of soul suicide. But when we know unworthiness is imagined, we are free to create and step outside of our self-imposed prisons.

For me, going public about the worth of every human being has taken me further into a space where unworthiness vs worthiness is no longer a legitimate question. If our thoughts and feelings were truth, they would be called facts. I have deep gratitude for the wisdom of this last sentence because I used to believe my self-demeaning thoughts and feelings. Now that I know thoughts and feelings are just energy in motion and part of our connection to our past, I have a deeper well to draw from when I coach or simply live my life.

By taking a stand for inherent worthiness, I have felt a powerful freedom and contentment. I am more embodied because my outside as a thought leader and coach match my inside as a human worthy of love, just like everyone else. These are some amazing benefits for someone who stumbled into a book writing retreat with no intention of writing a book, let alone becoming a thought leader with a mission.

Suzanne Longstreet

I'm Suzanne Longstreet and I'm the Millionaire Maker.

Over the past decade, I've coached many six-figure, action-oriented female entrepreneurs to blast through their limiting thought patterns, reprogram their minds for success, and achieve seven-figure revenues annually.

Through my work, I have empowered many women to break through their own glass ceilings and unlock their full potential. Using a combination of powerful techniques, including neuro-linguistic programming (NLP), hypnosis, positive intelligence, quantum linguistics, and Timeline Therapy Techniques TM, I guide clients to reprogram their unconscious minds and overcome the limiting beliefs and negative patterns that hold them back.

My journey hasn't always been easy. Like so many of us, I have struggled with imposter syndrome and the belief that I wasn't good enough. I simply refused to allow these limiting beliefs to hold me back and persevered to discover the best solutions to clear my mindset, and now I use my own experiences and learning to become even more powerful in my coaching practice.

My clients experience increased focus and clarity, and as a result, they charge more money for their services and confidently attract more clients.

Before my journey in the Thought Leader Academy, I was coaching clients one-on-one and quite happy with the people I was attracting and delighted with the results these clients were achieving. I had been attempting to write my second book and was really frustrated by my inability to find the time to write. Then I would doubt what I had written and wonder if there was a better way and a better process to follow to get my story, my thoughts, and my teachings out in the world. So, I chose to do nothing and just let my manuscript sit.

Since joining TLA, I've connected with my deeper reason for getting my book out in the world. It's still being written, and it is so much clearer to me why my particular message needs to be published and why only I can deliver this message. This is exciting to me as I can now see the book being published.

I've enjoyed meeting with and connecting with all of the amazing people in the Thought Leader Academy and watching them celebrate becoming award-winning and bestselling authors. This makes it feel so much more possible and probable to me that I too can be an award-winning and bestselling author. It's so much fun to hang out with these people who are mission driven and changing lives.

For me, my biggest celebration is finally launching the Quantum YOU program. This was a concept that I had been mulling over for years. After attending the Write and Grow Rich conference, I had a huge mindset shift. I realized that I had been playing small, only coaching one person in a session at a time. This led me to create the Quantum YOU program for six-figure entrepreneurs.

As a result of creating the Quantum YOU program, I've been able to share what I've learned with more women entrepreneurs and lead a community that is thriving. These clients are delighted with their results today.

Overall, I've really expanded my thinking, my mindset, my coaching business, and my circle of friends since joining the Thought Leader Academy. This program has given me so many joyful experiences and processes that work to grow myself and my business. The Thought Leader Academy offers so much more than any other program I've been in, and I am loving the sessions, conferences, and experiences.

As a result of Sara Connell's coaching and being in the Thought Leader Academy and Oracle Mastermind, my impact now goes far beyond my clients. As a champion of women's empowerment, I am building a community of like-minded women entrepreneurs who support each other in their journey to success in the Quantum YOU program. Today, the Quantum YOU program is changing lives, by facilitating female entrepreneurs across the world to shift their identities, behaviors, and patterns and achieve their desired outcomes.

With my commitment to continually evolving and expanding my offerings, I am now poised to guide even more women to achieve their dreams in the future.

Suzanne Longstreet, CPQC, TNLP, TCYF, TCHt
The Millionaire Maker

Clearing Your Muddled Thinking to Take Decisive Action & Increase Your Revenue

Success & Clarity Website = https://www.successandclarity.com/.

Sarah Vie

My first mantra or belief that changed everything for me in my life was something Sara Connell said to me when I first joined the Thought Leader Academy. The new idea of, "Do only what brings you joy."

My name is Sarah Vie and I have been a member of the Thought Leader Academy since its inception. This simple sentence has been my new identity throughout my journey working with Sara. I didn't realize that I could do that. I didn't realize I could give myself permission to slow down and only attract what I desired without any judgment or guilt. I only knew how to force myself to do things and I was doing so many things that I was burned out, exhausted, and I almost quit living in my purpose and showing others how to do the same.

I have now become a global abundance mentor helping countess woman release limited ancestral energy from their past and open to the limitless potential that we all have inside us. When this shift happens, they become "manifesting magnets."

With the guidance of Sara, I have written and released three bestselling and award-winning books. I have traveled the world with many of the women I mentor and facilitate abundance retreats, I have met the love of my life and continue building a loving, foundational relationship, and I have become a leader at five-star hotels leading meditation and abundance workshops. My latest manifestation has been creating Restorative Beach Rentals LLC, at my home in Rehoboth Beach, DE, filled with my new line of Restorative Foods, LLC, yummyhummusdaddy.com.

I encourage you to do the things that bring you joy. You too will be amazed at the creative energy you will feel in your soul. I am proof at the age of "sexty" I am living the most fulfilled and abundant life that I have ever lived. I feel flow, I feel ease, I feel clear in my vision.

Thank you to Sara and Thought Leader Academy, but I thank myself for believing that I can and I will.

You can check out my movement and books at: Sarahvie.com/magnet.

Amanda Hinman

I'm Amanda Hinman, a women's health expert and founder of Hinman Holistic Health where I help women to reclaim their health from hormone and gut imbalances such as hypothyroidism, autoimmune disease, insulin resistance, PCOS, anxiety, hypertension, and more so they can 3X their energy and mental clarity while optimizing weight.

When I started working with Sara, I'd just expanded my team because I was maxed out on the number of women I could serve and was not consistently sharing valuable content with my audience. I am deeply passionate about my mission to empower women to live inspired, knowledgeable, and to be confident about their health for the next ten, twenty, thirty, or even forty years.

I have worked with dozens of women who have reached a point of defeat when it comes to their health journey. Many have met with numerous doctors and medical professionals, have had a handful of lab work tests performed, and spent thousands of dollars on expensive supplements, and yet they still struggle with unwanted symptoms.

My unique approach combines functional medicine, root-cause resolution, and mindset training to help women develop the capacity to reorganize their minds, to shift their brain and nervous system for lasting health improvements.

The decision to expand my team and my impact was a huge deal for me because this meant I was committed to serving 10x more women. As a health consultant, I was doing really good work. My clients experienced incredible results, but I didn't know how to reach thousands of more women.

One of Sara's core teachings is sharing your expertise through thought leadership. This meant I put significant attention to communicating my message on a variety of platforms to impact more lives. I had to step out of my comfort zone. This meant committing to writing a book, pitching my mission to various groups, business leaders, and podcast hosts, offering free events to share my mission, and writing high-value content for my email list. There were many days I wanted to stay small and focus on my current clients only. I struggled with the belief that it was too hard and would take too much time to increase my visibility.

But as I kept carving out morning writing sessions, meeting with my editor, using the pitch templates, and receiving exceptional coaching from Sara and her team, my visibility did start to grow. In the past eighteen months, I have been interviewed on fifteen podcasts, hosted five four-day events, been a featured speaker at over twenty events and summits, increased my high-value writing to include an email every day, and expanded my audience significantly.

What's most important in all of this is what the commitment to my mission has allowed me to do.

I was able to break through the false belief that I wasn't a writer and wasn't able to be a thought leader who could positively empower thousands of women. Prior to this support, I didn't fully trust myself to show up and deliver consistently for 10x more women in our community. This massive step forward in leadership has forever changed what is possible for the business, for our clients, and for my family.

The expansion allowed me to collaborate with amazing team members who share my passion for empowering women to change their relationship with their bodies and feel confident in their long-term health. These women are amazing and love the work! They are talented and bring incredible expertise to our clients.

Most importantly, because of the persistence to follow TLA's techniques to increase our thought leadership, I've been able to serve and witness the life-changing impact of hundreds of women who now more deeply understand, appreciate, and support their health. This is what I was made to do, and it is deeply fulfilling work.

I believe that I received a divine intervention thirteen years ago when I was diagnosed with an auto-immune disease and my then eight-year-old daughter was experiencing daily seizures. We were told she would never be able to drive a car because of the amount of medication she required. Prior to that time, I had self-identified as very healthy and thought my daughter was too. However, this life redirection led me to embark on an educational journey that culminated in the study of over one hundred different dietary theories, three years of functional medicine science certification, and advanced psychological training in the latest behavior change technologies. I created Hinman Holistic Health as a way to pay it forward for my daughter's and my amazing health transformations. I want every woman to be inspired by the incredible potential within themselves for living vibrantly! This is why working with Sara Connell and Thought Leader Academy has been such a gift.

Please find out more at https://hinman-holistic.squarespace.com.

Lisa Taylor

I'm Lisa Taylor, author and founder of This Choice Matters, where I help successful people harness spiritual intuition and divine power with scientific certainty to heal problems in their careers, health, finances, and relationships.

After only six months in business, I saw the impact this science was making with my clients. I wanted to get the word out to a larger audience and see more high-performing, heart-centered individuals, who know they are meant for more, dramatically improve their confidence, consistency, and ability to trust their intuition and live by divine law and find a better quality of life, health, and fulfillment of purpose. To speak to a broader audience and have greater impact, I needed to write a book.

I loved my work and was finding great success with my clients, but for as long as I had an idea to write a book (having collected countless potential book titles over the years), I hadn't actually written a single page. I could talk all day, but I didn't see a clear path to publishing a book. I joined Thought Leader Academy and started working with Sara.

One of Sara's core teachings is "you can and you will" and in the very first book-writing workshop I took of Sara's, she said writing a book comes down to my making the decision to do it. In that session, I made a commitment to finish the book. In Sara's community of thought leaders, I got ongoing support from Sara and other members who saw my strength and clear vision and affirmed, "You can and you will," because, as Sara says, "There's a way. There's a way. There's always a way." With the clarity of Sara's message, her vision for each of her members, her methodical proven strategies, and the incredible community of individuals modeling success, I wrote my first book.

When I was eighteen, I found myself floating above my body choosing to stay or go. And the reason I returned to my body and stayed on the planet was to share the incredible truth I'd seen. Forty years later, I still hadn't fulfilled my life's commitment. I hadn't told the truth to those who needed to hear it. Writing the book with the support of TLA honed my core message and solidified my purpose on the planet. Now I can affect change in the lives of anyone who will make the choice to harness the power of divine intuition and trust that divine law is operating in their life and the scientific inevitable results they will see in their own experience. You have the same choice to live by divine law, follow the intuition you have within, to live with the confidence, consistency, and courage to be who you were made to be and commit to live the life you've always dreamed of. The process is easy and the results are scientifically assured.

I am now a bestselling author and international speaker, affecting thousands of lives all over the world. Aside from Sara's expert guidance in writing, publishing, and marketing my book, her understanding and training in the area of abundance has shifted my money mindset, freed me from limiting beliefs, and allowed me to see my true worth and charge more accurately for my services. While working with Sara, I've doubled my membership, taken on high-end private clients, and doubled my monthly income, all while following my calling and doing what I love.

Because I have honed my message through this process of writing the book, I more quickly reach the people for whom my message is beneficial, and I'm able to serve on a larger scale. My clients have found freedom from addiction, psychosis, wheelchair use, migraines, arthritis, cancer, lack of purpose, depression, anxiety, fear of flying, flu, Covid, high and low blood pressure, hoarding (just to name a few). Members of This Choice Matters experience healing, find their purpose, feel fulfilled, trust their intuition and inner guidance, feel confident, and worthy of living their best life without fear.

My mission is for you to choose to be a spiritual warrior and put infinite power at the center of every decision in your life and lean on scientific divine law to govern your career, wealth, health, and relationships.

You can find out more at www.thischoicematters.co.

Julie Fedeli and Pamela DeRose

We are Julie Fedeli and Pamela DeRose, dedicated to supporting women in living their very best lives. We are the founders of Midlife Upgrade, bestselling authors and creators of an online community and educational platform to help women navigate their midlife journey. Each of us has been an advocate for women's health and wellness for over thirty years, offering our love and expertise.

We were invited to one of Sara Connell's retreats almost a year ago. We made a deal with each other, and said, "We aren't buying anything!" We decided that if we didn't love it, we would quietly exit at lunchtime. The morning began with a video about female authors that blew our minds, and then Sara came on stage. About one minute into Sara's presentation, Pam and I looked at each other with tears in our eyes, and we knew we were goners! Sara was the REAL DEAL. We were the first two to enroll in her fabulous, year-long Thought Leader Academy, which has paid for itself many times over.

We had a vague idea of what we were hoping to create to empower women during menopause, but we had a very clear intention to uplift the conversation about midlife and aging. We had the awareness during the retreat that we had been thought leaders for women's health for decades, but we had never considered writing a book. With the guidance of Sara and her team, we have written a bestselling book, and have created a magical, online learning platform that is transforming women's lives.

Participating in Sara's community has exponentially shortened the learning curve for us, and gently encouraged us to move way beyond our former comfort zones. And we are now living examples for our readers, clients, and our community of midlife women, and have upgraded our lives with the Thought Leader Academy as the foundation for our personal and professional growth.

We envision our movement rippling out all over the planet, creating an elevated midlife experience for women and subsequent generations. We hope to align with movements adjacent to ours, and blow up the fucking patriarchy and make a shit ton of money in the process!!!

Midlifeupgrade.com.

Michelle Thames

Hello! I am Michelle Thames, a marketing and monetization strategist with a core mission of empowering women entrepreneurs. I've dedicated myself to helping them increase their visibility, attract more clients, and leverage their expertise for profitability. My journey in the entrepreneurial realm was a complex one. I was laid off from a healthcare job in 2016, but instead of seeing it as a setback, I viewed it as an opportunity to ignite my passions. My experiences as an influencer over the past fourteen years and my effective use of social media landed me a coveted role in digital marketing for a leading beauty brand. There, I helped lay the foundational bricks of their business in the digital space. This valuable experience led me to establish my marketing agency alongside my husband and a coaching and consulting business. Together, we bid farewell to our nine-to-five jobs to chase our dreams wholeheartedly.

I had amassed a following when I joined TLA, yet my message could have been more straightforward. I needed clarification about my target audience and had yet to venture into hosting large-scale online events. While thriving in many ways, I knew I was standing on the precipice of a significant transformation, ready to level up. TLA became the catalyst for this much-needed change.

The *S-S-S* method is one of the most impactful strategies I've adopted from TLA. This technique has provided the structure and clarity I needed to outline my upcoming book-a project I am incredibly excited about! Sara's approach to imparting knowledge through practical advice and her effortless teaching style has been a game changer for me. As I write these words, the reality that I will soon be a published author fills me with an overwhelming sense of accomplishment.

Of the many things I've created, I hold immense pride in the two online summits I hosted this year. These events attracted thousands of registrations and maintained a steady flow of live attendees daily. The energy and engagement at these virtual summits were remarkable, and I eagerly anticipate the experience of hosting my first in-person event.

As for the future, my aspirations are high. I am eager to take my work to new heights as a thought leader, particularly with my forthcoming book and increasing speaking engagements. My dream is to travel the world and share my knowledge of marketing and monetization with women globally. There's also my podcast, *Social Media Decoded*, which already enjoys a global audience. I aim to nurture its growth and reach even further corners of the world.

Join me on this exciting journey and become part of my movement. Follow me on Instagram at www.instagram.com/michellelthames to stay updated with my projects and access a wealth of resources to empower women entrepreneurs.

Nancy Linnerooth

I'm Nancy Linnerooth, founder of the MVP Activator, where women business owners come to get rid of their subconscious blocks so they can make more money, become more visible, and get more support. I do that using EFT, or "Tapping." Over and over again, clients have told me that our work together has changed their lives.

My mission is to get rid of what's been holding women leaders back so they can finally create the lives, the businesses, and the impact they are meant to have.

When I first joined TLA, I knew my mission. I'd already built a business and helped many clients. I had even started creating a large group program—my MVP Activator—that would allow me to serve more women.

Yet I knew I was called to do more. Much more. For that I needed to finish the MVP Activator, then write a book to get my message out in a much bigger way.

It had been on my to-do list for seven years to write that book! I knew it would start by letting women entrepreneurs know there's nothing wrong with them if they procrastinate or even sabotage their own efforts. It would go on to explain about the subconscious blocks that are keeping them stuck. Finally, it would walk them through my step-by-step process to release those blocks.

Seven years after realizing I needed to write that book, though, I still hadn't written a word of it.

The MVP Activator was nearly up and running when I joined TLA, but there were still several large features I needed to create to give my clients their full transformation. I figured the book would just have to wait until after I finished building out the program.

With Sara Connell's coaching, I was able to rethink that plan. She showed me several techniques to fit writing into my extremely busy schedule. Particularly useful were her "writing wedges"—small blocks of time in between other commitments I could use to write. I finally started writing that book I'd been talking about for so long.

It was easier than I expected. Sara and her team kept me focused and on track with their amazing support. They also gave me encouragement and advice as I launched the MVP Activator.

I'm proud to say the first draft of my book is nearly finished. And I was able to write it while continuing to serve my clients and grow my program.

With the help of Sara and TLA, I'm now much closer to my vision of helping all the women I'm called to serve through my MVP Activator and my (almost finished) book.

Our world needs more women in leadership positions. With their mindset, visibility, and profitability blocks gone, women entrepreneurs can fully step into being the leaders that their businesses, their families, and their industries need.

Then they will change our world in the ways that only they can.

To find out whether you have subconscious blocks and get my three free tap-along videos to release common subconscious blocks, take the short quiz at www.UnblockResults.com/TLA.

Shari Biery

"Do you have a book in you?" The question pierced through my doubts and insecurities, leaving me in disbelief. Writing a book was something I never, ever considered for myself. But something shifted within me when Sara Connell, a guest speaker in my mastermind group, posed that thought-provoking question. It was as if Sara saw a spark in me, a potential I had never recognized.

As Sara shared her life story, filled with its own share of twists, setbacks, and triumphs, her words resonated deep within my soul. The power of a book to transform lives became evident as she spoke about how it had saved her own. Then, I began to see the immense impact a book could have on my mission and the change I wanted to bring to the world. Sara reminded me of Toni Morrison's powerful quote, "If there's a book that you want to read, but it hasn't been written yet, then you must write it." Suddenly, writing a book wasn't just a distant dream—it was a call to action.

With Sara's guidance and support, I accepted the invitation to join the Thought Leader Academy. As a veteran military spouse and National Board certified health and wellness coach, I knew I had a unique perspective to share. I understood the challenges military spouses and families face, and I was passionate about helping them prioritize their own well-being and find fulfillment amidst the demands of military life. My mission is to empower women to embrace their true selves, transform their relationships with time, body, and self-worth, and live purposeful lives.

Being a part of the Thought Leader Academy community under Sara's powerful coaching has been a transformative journey. Not only have I grown personally and professionally, but I have also been able to create new offerings that cater to the specific needs of my clients. Through the Abundance Accelerator, I developed the Thirty-Day Jump Start to Nourish You Program, providing a structured framework for women to kickstart their health and well-being journey. Additionally, I established a group membership that offers continued coaching support and accountability in prioritizing self-care.

But it doesn't stop there. Through the Thought Leader Academy, I have had incredible opportunities to increase my visibility and amplify my impact. As a paid speaker, I have stood before audiences, empowering women to say "yes" to themselves and their well-being. The support and encouragement from Sara, along with the unwavering belief of my editors, Hannah and Audrey, have fueled my determination to complete my manuscript. I am now in the final editing stages, eagerly awaiting its release in the coming year. I can't wait to witness the transformations it brings and the messages it shares with women worldwide.

The friendships and benefits I have gained from being part of the Thought Leader Academy community are immeasurable. The unwavering support and camaraderie of like-minded women have been instrumental in my growth. With accountability buddies by my side, cheering me on, I have pushed past self-limiting beliefs and embraced new possibilities. I have realized that I am not alone on this journey in this compassionate and empowering community. Together, we are a force supporting, uplifting, and valuing each other as women, creating a world where individuals feel empowered to prioritize their dreams and live their unique stories.

I am forever grateful for the opportunities and growth that being part of the Thought Leader Academy community has brought into my life. It has allowed me to serve others more effectively while finding the support and inspiration I need to shine brighter. As we say in TLA, "You Can and You Will!"

If you'd like to learn more about my mission and connect with me, visit www.sharibiery.com.

Shari Biery

THOUGHT LEADER ACADEMY

National Board Certified Health and Wellness Coach
Alive With Purpose Health and Life Coaching, LLC

Esther Avant

I'm Esther Avant, sports nutritionist, personal trainer, and creator of the Gone For Good formula for weight loss that lasts. I help busy professional women lose weight for the last time through a combination of exercise, nutrition, mindset, and lifestyle related coaching.

When I started with Sara, I had finished the first draft of my book using a DIY course from another coach, but I couldn't imagine that mess turning into an actual book that would provide the kind of impact I was envisioning and had no idea how to make it better.

Through Sara's ongoing coaching, diving into the wealth of resources available in the TLA portal, and attending my first in-person event with Sara's company, I developed the confidence to know that I do have what it takes to publish a book I'm proud of, and that helps hundreds of women lose weight for the last time. Sara helped me realize that the only difference between me and the authors I admire is that they've already done the work to create the books. Much like I coach my own clients to do, all I have to do is follow the road map and trust the process and I, too, will be a published author!

I appreciate that Sara coaches the whole person, not just the tiny segment of our lives that relates to writing and speaking. Every time I attend a coaching call with a question or concern, Sara helps me get clarity and inspires me to continue taking action.

One of the most valuable aspects of TLA for me has been the sessions with an editor. Because I came into the program with my book already written, I was able to jump right in and start taking advantage of working with a professional to make my book the best it can possibly be. The insights I've gotten and improvements I've made as a result have already improved the book immensely.

I'm very proud of being on the verge of having a completed manuscript! Within a couple of weeks of writing this, I will be sending it off to a handful of beta readers, making a final round of edits, and sending it to the publisher!

I'm excited to release my book into the world, grow my coaching business, and begin tackling in-person speaking events as my next challenge!

If you're interested in learning more about me and what I do, check out my podcast called *Live Diet-Free*. If you have a weight loss goal, make sure to download my Weight Loss That Lasts Cheat Sheet to learn the three-part formula I've used to help hundreds of women lose weight for the last time. You can get it at www.estheravant.com/cheatsheet.

Amy Gibson

I'm Amy Gibson, author, activist, speaker, and founder of The Girl in a Tree Life Coaching where I guide women through transformational energy work to reach higher awareness in their lives to climb higher in their tree of life.

When I started working with Sara, it was right when Covid hit. I was just graduating from an intensive accreditation coaching program. Through this training, many of my colleagues learned about my unusual life experiences and urged me to write a memoir about my life-saving connection with nature and how I became a tree climber of life. One of my colleagues was a member of Sara Connell's Thought Leadership Academy and invited me to the virtual retreat. This is where I solidified my calling to write my memoir and share my story and inspire others to reclaim their connection with nature.

Combining both my life-coaching skills with ecotherapy, I created a mission of empowering women to live a more conscious, connected life through nature. My passion is rooted in guiding people to new awakenings, to heal through nature, and to reach higher branches in all areas in their lives.

Without hesitation, I joined TLA during the virtual retreat in 2020 and haven't looked back. I knew that I needed to invest in myself and my vision. My intuition kicked in and I knew that Sara was the coach who was going to guide me to success. I went to every one of Sara's training and coaching sessions, soaking in her vast knowledge and resources like a tree soaking in water from its roots. Thanks to her training on how to build a community, I now have a growing Facebook community, Amy's Treehouse Club, where I share my personal connection to nature and guide others on how to reconnect to nature easily each day.

Thanks to Sara's highly motivating and supportive courses, I also now have a completed manuscript that has been approved by Muse Literary Publishing House. I am continuing to embrace all of Sara's courses such as the Abundance Accelerator and How to Monetize Your Mission. Where I can release and proclaim myself in a higher vibration and show up in my life as a leader and guide in all aspects of my life.

Sara's community of amazing women has been a huge support system and a major part of life today. I have a huge network of friends, colleagues, and cohorts because I choose to attend each of her retreats. They brought me clarity, joy, and resources that I never would have found all on my own.

Through this experience I have become the woman who honors the wisdom that the girl in a tree was born knowing. My mission in this lifetime is to guide women to higher awareness in their lives, allowing them to reach higher branches in their tree of life. We are all tree climbers of life if we choose to climb! Passing along this deep knowledge to the next generation, creating shade from the seeds we plant today for the next generations to enjoy. You can find out more and receive a free guided tree grounding meditation at www.thegirlinatree.com, join my community on FB Amy's Treehouse Club, and connect with me on IG @thegirlinatreetx.

Kelly Lutman

I am Kelly Lutman, a health coach certified in applied functional medicine who helps people frustrated by what seems to be a life sentence in their chronic disease diagnosis. I help them identify the root causes of their disease and what their body needs to be able to function properly. More recently, I have begun to work with cancer patients to help them support the rest of their body, which can suffer collateral damage if it doesn't receive nourishment. The medical team is focused on the cancer, but too many patients have little guidance or empowerment in how to support their body through the journey.

When I first heard about Sara Connell and Thought Leader Academy, I had embarked on research for a book to provide guidance for cancer patients in nourishing the rest of their body while on their cancer journey. I had self-published a bestselling book many years before, but I wanted this new book to have a bigger impact and felt strongly that Sara was the one to inspire and guide me. What I didn't realize I would also receive was the tremendous energy of the members of Thought Leader Academy-from ideas, to encouragement, and examples of what was possible; the rising tide of TLA raises all boats.

Thriving Through Cancer: A Whole-istic Approach for Your Journey has been released and is a bestseller. On the wave of its very favorable reception, I am looking forward to offering an online membership support group to provide guidance and build community for those on a cancer journey. The book itself can benefit those who don't have cancer, as well as those who have a diagnosis-get a copy at www.KellyLutman.com.

Joan Coletto

Hello! My name is Joan Coletto, and I am a dedicated spiritual practitioner and advanced clinical hypnotherapist. I have made it my mission and devoted my life to empowering individuals to unlock their own potential, overcome obstacles, and align with their highest vision for a fulfilling life.

Almost two decades ago, I first met Sara, watching in admiration as she relentlessly carved out her path and built TLA. When the invitation came for Women Starting Movements in 2022, my intuition was crystal clear . . . I needed to be there. Having advocated the importance of trusting one's gut and inner voice with my clients, it was time to practice what I preach.

The buzz, camaraderie, and genuine support at the conference was extraordinary. As I left, a powerful sense of clarity enveloped me . . . I had found the trajectory for my book and an incredible network that would celebrate me in this journey as I celebrated theirs. The honor of sharing space with ambitious women committed to creating impactful movements was transformative.

A standout strategy I discovered through TLA was the win-win-win mindset. It dawned on me that my mission to empower others rippled out to affect more than I could immediately see. As I grew in visibility and shared my book with the world, each reader's life I could touch, in turn, influenced others around them . . . a domino effect of positive change.

One of my favorite TLA gems that revolutionized my process was 'pleasure bundling.' Combining an initially unpalatable task, such as a difficult writing stint with a delightful activity, transformed my approach and helped me flow back into the rhythm of writing at times when I felt stuck.

Stepping out of my comfort zone in TLA has propelled me further than I'd ever imagined. I've set and met ambitious goals and deadlines, sparking a renewed excitement in my work. This has had a rippling effect on my clients as well.

As I put the final touches on my book, I am brimming with excitement for the launch of my online subscription group. This platform will allow me to expand my reach, offering more individuals access to workshops, classes, meditation and hypnosis recordings, as well as live coaching and Q&A sessions.

Slated for release in early spring of 2024, my book is a beacon of hope and a guide brimming with practical insights on living a joyous, abundant life. I look forward to connecting with you, as together we unlock the path to an empowered life.

For more details about my work, please visit my website at www.joancoletto.com.

Kate Furnish

I, Kate Furnish, am a practicing physical therapist and women's empowerment coach.

As a physical therapist who has worked in pediatrics, orthopedics, home health, and specializes in myofascial release body work, I am dedicated to how bodies develop, function, grow, and heal. My goal is your empowered movement for life, mind, body, and spirit. After two decades teaching principles of wellness and healing alongside physical therapy, I realized the information I was sharing needed to be put into form. In 2014, I wrote a healing journal to help people on their healing journey. It is a place to connect to yourself and record and track your journey of healing and well-being. Recently in 2022, I went a step further and developed a coaching program featuring what I have coined the Joy Mastery Method™ to experience joy and fulfillment now. Healing is coming into your body, feeling, releasing, making space for your presence. Living is coming into your life through the body with the presence of your soul, your unique self. I know this is your source of strength, magic, and fulfillment.

I have seen too many women, with generous loving hearts, manage it all and secretly wonder when it's their turn to enjoy life. These women are trying so hard to get it "right," they sometimes forget to check in with their own hearts regarding what is actually right for them personally. Survivors are often good at over-functioning and putting their own needs aside. What I have learned through my own healing journey, as well as working with thousands of others through physical therapy and body work, is that connecting to what we need helps us to know ourselves and is essential to a good life.

It turns out when we care for and ask for our needs, we are not selfish, we are generous. Imagine if all your needs were met, physical, emotional, spiritual, mental, would you be more or less generous with others from this place? Yes, you answer, "more generous" because that is already who you are. If you've ever felt selfish asking for what you need, now is the time to change this. When you thrive, the world receives more you, and that is the best gift you have to offer the world.

As a result of working with me, women activate their soul presence and experience joy and fulfillment now. Women learn simple practices to take up space in the day-to-day moments of life, staking a claim for their own life. No more waiting until the list is done or things are settled or until you've gotten it all right. Life is NOW. I have created a group coaching program for women to come together and support each other, to be and express the soul of who they are. What could be more delicious than practicing presence and joy with others in a group dedicated to each member thriving in her unique way and shining her brilliant light?

This coaching program is what inspired me to join Thought Leader Academy, to gain support to write my book. I am writing to bring these principles to more and more women. I am on a mission to unlock joy in the hearts of people around the world.

Thought Leader Academy is a group of authors with mission in the world, coming together to support one another, to write and share those missions. They are a high-vibe community practicing principles of spiritual truth, who care about divine alignment and making the world a better place with the soul mission they have received. It is wonderful to step into this community and receive support for my mission and be inspired by others. This was a gift I gave myself.

The world has been in a hard press lately. Perhaps this is nothing new; part of life's journey is running the gauntlet of challenges before us. There is also a spiritual awakening happening. I believe we are at a choice point in history. To belong to a community that is dedicated to empowerment, possibility, and making the world a better place through its writing is to be rich indeed. To have this community cheering me on and blazing the path is priceless.

I have a vision of each of us rising to the challenge of our lives, using our voice to express who we are and what we have learned or created, shining our light, and enjoying our lives. What will the world look and feel like when we are all free and safe to do this?

I am so proud that in 2023, since joining Thought Leader Academy, I will be featured in a book coming out August 8 of 2023 called *Unlocking the Matrix: The New Codes of Ancient Egypt* compiled by Corrina Steward and Paula Jessop. It felt scary to write and wonder if what I had to say was relevant, to reveal myself vulnerably and honestly, to create something new. And it was powerfully freeing and empowering to speak my story, to share my voice, to create something new, and see it take shape before my eyes. Our lives are also our creation, our co-creation with the divine flowing through and guiding and inspiring us. What an adventure!

I invite and encourage you to claim your life today. Accept what is, dream for what you desire, and start playing, creating, and having some fun (even when you're doing dishes).

If you'd like to connect with me, let's get to know each other: https://katefurnish.as.me/PurityCodesActivation.

Lisa Deck

I'm Lisa Deck, a licensed clinical social worker and certified intuitive eating counselor. I am passionate about helping women break free from diet culture and rediscover their own self-trust. I am the leader behind the Welcoming Every Body™ movement and the founder of Embody Collective, an anti-diet, pro-feminism community. We believe that every body deserves respect, and our purpose is to provide support and alliance to women learning to nourish themselves intuitively and reclaim body freedom.

Joining Thought Leader Academy was a twist of fate. I ended up at one of Sara's inspiring retreats after following a gut feeling that maybe I was supposed to be there. What started as a dream to someday write a book turned into a fire for sharing the message of intuitive eating far and wide and an unshakeable belief that I was the one to do it. While I was there, deciding if I could afford to invest in the program, a current member (who I did not know before the retreat started), told me that she believed I had something important to share with the world. She offered to pay my deposit to join the community if I was ready to take that next step. Ready or not, I believe in having the courage to walk through doors that open for you!

That first experience with Thought Leader Academy has resonated throughout my time in the program. Sara always says, "The answer is in the room." And I have found that being "in the room" with leaders who have been where I want to go and are genuinely happy to support me has made all the difference. I recently heard a speaker use the phrase "midwife my dream" with regard to her support system, and my first thought was, *Yes! That is exactly what Sara and my TLA community have done for me this year!* I started my journey with a blurry dream and a nudge from a future-focused new friend. Over the course of the year, miracles have dropped in and opportunities have come together to allow that dream to come to fruition.

So many things Sara says stick with me, but one of them is, "What if it gets to be easy?" And that's what I've experienced this year in Thought Leader Academy. With just the right amount of accountability and the buoyancy of a rising tide, each step has felt easy, even fun, in a way that I never expected it could. With Sara's guidance, I've been so clear on the next right thing at each stage of starting my business and writing my book that I've been able to truly enjoy the process.

While Embody Collective is still in its early season and my book is still in development, I can see ahead to where we're going and I am thrilled by what's unfolding! It gets to be easy, and fun, and meaningful and impactful. With the confidence that I've gained from being a part of this group, I know that not only is my mission possible, but that the world is waiting for it. Together, we will dismantle the cultural messages that tell women that they must remain small and instead empower women to expand their vision and live fully in alignment with their values.

If our movement resonates with you, please join us! Every body is welcome. www.welcomingeverybody.com.

Rachel Ledet

I'm Rachel Ledet, marketing strategist and change agent for small to medium-sized businesses. I work with organizations with five to two hundred employees to establish their brand messaging, communications planning, outreach activities, and establishing an intentional corporate culture. I absolutely love working alongside the leadership team to learn the ins and outs of their business, but most importantly how their people work, and what makes them thrive as individuals. Marketing is the simple act of creating a plan and communicating well to your targeted audience. My company, 30|90 Marketing, ensures that whatever communication is needed to grow or change your organization to meet your desired outcomes, we're here to guide you in the practical steps and appropriate language to get you there.

When I met Sara Connell and was introduced to Thought Leadership Academy, I was already in a phase I call "the winds of change." I had an urging and a sort of pull for almost a year telling that it was time to step up beyond my comfort zone to grow my business. I also had a deep desire to take my casual content writing and formalized curriculum writing and transform my work into a book, but I didn't know which story I would tell or how I would start. I attended a TLA conference in New Orleans, and within a few hours, I knew that Sara's vibe spoke to me. She was smart and seasoned but so approachable and warm. What really struck me was her delivery, which I was waiting for, of her package offering. She offered to take you wherever you wanted to go–expand your brand, become a national speaker, write a book, build a program. It was a structured enough plan to get you there but flexible enough to allow you to follow your own vision. It was there that I confirmed my decision to write a book and knew that TLA was the vehicle to get me there. Sara offered a mentor and a roadmap, and I was in!

My favorite practices learned from TLA are to really future-pull what you want something to be. Sara's exercise to discover what my future self needs from this book really helped me decide on the story I was wanting to tell, who my audience was supposed to be, and why I was so sure I needed to write this book this way. In my coaching session with Alex, I was able to talk freely about my thoughts, how I approach things, why I care about my clients so much, and what outcomes I can bring for them. She listened thoughtfully and very clearly helped me to establish the three main themes or pillars for my book. The second technique that has helped me get to the next step is story mapping. For me this meant taking my three pillars and jotting down each part that needed to be in that special section. Sara's coaching has guidelines and frameworks for how to get there but is loose enough to include off-shoots if they work for your book. Not only does she encourage this, she helps you figure it out! With each group call and personal coaching session, I come away with new ideas but most importantly a to-do list of exactly HOW to do it. This is what makes all the difference to me. TLA promises a roadmap, and Sara and her team show up with all the tools to get you there. You just have to apply yourself and decide to get your words on the page.

So far I'm most proud of creating my story map because I know that I can take this homework and slowly chip away at it until I have something for my editor to review. I'm also proud of how I have carved out more time in my week to think through these things and to get creative with my thoughts. I'm working to build in even more writing and brainstorming time so that I can get the first few chapters written.

My ultimate goal is to use my book as a vehicle to connect with businesses around the country to help them develop marketing strategies that really work. By establishing myself as a public speaker, published writer, and curriculum builder, I can teach and demonstrate the ways to orchestrate branding, culture, and communications in ways that are authentic and impactful. Too many companies see their employees as cogs in their wheel instead of pouring into them as their greatest asset. My marketing strategies combine external and internal communications so that everybody wins.

My website is www.3090marketing.com. (I may add some book-related resources, but they aren't here yet!)

Shelley Brown

I have been writing a book called, *Moving Up Without Sucking Up*–how to move ahead in the corporate world without sacrificing your personal values for a number of years, but I didn't really know what to do with it. I attended Sara's Thought Leader Academy event, Write and Grow Rich, in New Orleans in May 2023 and, suddenly, everything came together for me during this retreat; it all fell into place and made sense. I left there with a renewed passion and a solid road map on how to finish my book, how to get it edited, and how to get it published. Even more than the book, the retreat sparked a fire in me that had been dormant for a few years, I was energized about my work, future possibilities, and life in general. A friend asked me, "How was the retreat?" My answer was "life changing."

What makes some people successful where others fail? What are the qualities that are needed to succeed in the corporate world? So many people have tried to figure this out–my mission is to provide a blueprint to being seen as a "high potential" employee.

I have worked in human resources my whole career for big, multi-national companies; I became a vice president of human resources at thirty-four years old; I started my own consulting firm at forty-two years old; I sold my consulting firm at fifty-four years old. I have a degree in psychology, I am a professional coach, certified in lots of psychometric testing, completed the Wharton Business Leadership Certificate and was named as one of Canada's Distinctive Women.

I have my own small business again, Ninebox HR (www.nineboxhr.ca). A nine-box grid is a way of looking at employees by discussing not only their performance in their current role, but their potential for future roles or projects. I know that I can help guide young corporate employees to become the person in the upper right-hand box, an exceed expectations performer with high potential in the next one to two years of their career.

Since the Write and Grow Rich retreat, I have attended a book writing intensive over three days, have participated in a pod of like-minded authors, and have been connected to my writing coach. This is exactly what I was looking for in order to keep me focused, hold me accountable, and give me the support I needed to finally move towards my goal.

An exercise that we did was called a Future Pull. We each took five Post-it notes, and put *P* on the first, *C* on the second, *M1* on the third, *M2* on the fourth and *VF* on the fifth. *C* is for current, and we started there, thinking about our individual current state, getting a clear picture in our mind of where we were relative to our goal. I thought of the work I had put into my book so far, what was good about it, how much I had achieved. *P* is for past, an opportunity to step back and think about the past and what was accomplished in the past to bring us to this current state. I thought about how much more experience I had gained since starting the book and how much more valuable content I can now add. We moved back to *P* for present state. Then stepped forward to *M1* for the first milestone to get us to the Future State. I chose a twelve-month timeline for the first milestone, which was finishing the writing and editing portion of my book. I have a clear picture in my mind of where I will be, how I will feel, and the celebration dinner afterward! Now we stepped forward to *M2*, the second milestone. I chose a six-month timeline (from *M1*), and I pictured receiving the box of books after it was delivered to my front door, pulling open the box, and taking out the first copy. The last step is *VF* for Vivid Future state. I clearly saw myself coming out on stage as a keynote speaker at a large conference, asking the audience, "Who is here to advance in their career without sucking up to anyone?"; and the audience claps and is ready to hear my fun and thought-provoking presentation. We did the exercise six times, each time reinforcing it in our minds. I have always been a fan of visualization, but this gave structure and made it even more powerful.

Overall, I found joining the Thought Leadership Academy energizing, positive, and motivating. Look for my book to be ready for purchase in June 2024!!

Camille Winer

I'm Camille Winer, one of the cofounders of Yodelpop, Inc., a marketing solutions firm dedicated to assisting mission-driven organizations harness the power of marketing and amplify their impact in creating a more sustainable world.

Up until last year, despite a consistent career path, business, and multiple degrees, I still felt invisible in the business world and had persistent imposter syndrome that plagued me as an entrepreneur. I was experiencing what Sara calls 'business dysmorphia'–deep down inside, I identified more with a kid running a lemonade stand than a successful entrepreneur. I felt there was more I could contribute to the world, but I didn't know how to bring it forth.

TLA STORIES

I decided to attend Sara's Women Starting Movements retreat with my business partner.

Having known Sara for years within personal circles, I had witnessed her remarkable journey as she fearlessly embarked on her path to building a thriving empire as a writer and coach. Her authenticity, grace, generous spirit, and unwavering courage have inspired me. Seeing her conquer self-limiting beliefs and behaviors to share her gifts and make a positive difference in the world has been truly awe-inspiring.

Since embarking on a journey in Thought Leader Academy, I no longer feel like a stuck entrepreneur. TLA has equipped me with the tools to expand my capacity to handle the paralyzing doubts and nagging fears that plagued me for years. I'm learning to become more comfortable being uncomfortable by taking consistent action further outside of my comfort zone.

In 2017, I completed a sustainable MBA program, and upon graduation, I was eager to transform my graduate thesis into a tangible contribution towards society and the growth of our agency. However, I was uncertain about the form it should take and whether it would be worth pursuing. With the assistance of TLA, I've begun the process of converting my research into a book that explores the establishment of an unwavering marketing culture amidst the challenges of disruption and connectivity in today's world.

My vision extends beyond just the expansion of my previous research, as I intend to incorporate insights and expertise from my business partner, combining our collective experiences. Together, we will collaborate on publishing the book, launching a podcast, speaking and developing a program that will amplify our impact and engage with our target audience.

We've launched a new brand that emerged from the TLA network: FollowUp Marketing helps coaches, consultants, and solopreneurs market efficiently and effectively with a suite of empowering solutions. Feel free to explore our offerings at followup-marketing.com/TLA. Additionally, you can discover our nonprofit marketing solutions at yodelpop.com/TLA.

I am happy to say that passing a lemonade stand no longer evokes limiting beliefs about myself and my capabilities. Instead, I smile as I know I'm on a solid path of embracing my identity as a successful entrepreneur and influential visionary. I have experienced greater depths of my creativity, and I feel excited to continue the journey.

Tess Vaughn

Hello all, I am Tess Vaughn. I have been a physical therapist for twenty-seven years and have helped thousands of clients through the years. The best way to describe the end goal of each person I see, no matter their diagnosis or what part of their body I may be working on, is I help others find their JOY.

Think about what it feels like to have pain or limitations. The pain can be acute like a low back or hip pain that happens after doing a heavy squat lift or maybe it's more chronic and it catches you every time you try to do something. It may not be a high level of pain, but it sits there with you as you try to exercise or live your life. Maybe you're a runner or Cross Fitter who leaks with exercise or a new mom who just wants her body to feel strong and stable again. Possibly you are young and just starting a relationship, but being intimate with your partner is painful.

I see you and I've been there myself. It's exhausting and it steals your joy. You lose confidence in your body and in yourself. You choose to "take it easy" instead of going for a run or meeting your friends at the gym. You start to pull away from your partner because the thought of intimacy becomes overwhelming. All of this may be common, but it's not normal and it doesn't have to be something you just live with.

Through the support, guidance, and information available through TLA, it is my mission to reach women who are choosing "safe" over JOY and to help them find their confidence again. I have just submitted my first draft of my first book! It is a children's book on finding personal joy through the eyes and adventures of a duck named Edith.

TLA has taught me how to push myself, while being supported, and to have bigger dreams. To reach more people, not for self-aggrandization, but to share an important message that someone, right now, needs to hear. As TLA guides me through the process of writing my first book, I already have plans for the next book!

TLA and the ladies I have learned from and listened to for the last three months have also reminded me of the worth of my knowledge, experience, and words. I have been able to more than double my monthly income each month for the last three months as compared to last year by feeling confident to raise my prices, make the offer every day, and to understand I would be doing a disservice to others if I didn't share my knowledge or let someone know how I can help them.

Email: tess@ptliveit.com.

YouTube channel: @tessvaughn.

Instagram: https://instagram.com/ptliveit.

Wendee Villanueva

I am Wendee Villanueva, author, speaker, and BrainPlay coach (neuro-somatic intelligence). I help women to calm their nervous system, so they can move out of anxiety and overwhelm into sustainable peace and create a peaceful life that they love.

I first met Sara in a leadership program, where we were put as strangers into a breakout room and told to yell the question, "What do you want?!?!" at each other. It was intense and her passion brought me to tears. She has since created everything that she declared on that day. Since I joined TLA, Sara has continued to evoke this question within me of what I want. When I entered the program, I had a portion of my mother's memoir written that I kept tightly guarded, as I continued to strive for perfection and protect my vulnerability in this very personal book.

Through Sara's encouragement and my incredible editor, I wrote my heart out. Throughout my time in TLA, I was stretched to own my talents, my power, my voice, and my worth. Writing brought out my dreams, my fears, imposter syndrome, and amplified the feelings that I was experiencing in my life. Sara guided us through future pulling exercises, which stretched me to envision myself making an impact in the world far beyond what I could have imagined. When she guided us through exercises stepping farther and farther into our future, my future enticed me forward. I feared standing still more than I did making potential mistakes and growing. When obstacles arise with my book or in life, Sara's words echo in my heart. I have two favorites: "There's a way. There's a way. There's always a way," and "I can and I will!" My book now contains my mom's story, as well as my own. I am in the process of final edits. I began my own business, started speaking to groups of women, and began a second book! I have met and collaborated with some of the most amazing women in TLA, and I now know that I belong at the table!

I am most proud of completing my book and the growth and perseverance that I have modeled for my daughters in the process.

I am excited to complete my second book and to inspire women to speak their truth, live a life they are proud of, and to remind them that there is always a way.

www.wendeeleann.com.

Amy Day

I'm Amy Day and I'm on a mission to help people get out of decision fatigue, overwhelm, and the paralyzing fear of making the wrong choice by teaching them HOW to make great decisions. The truth is we make about 35,000 decisions a day and can spend more than three hours making them.

Your most valuable resource is time and yet how much of yours is wasted in the swirl of indecision?

Your life is created by your choices and you are the decision maker! So why do you get stuck? There is a better way to make decisions that you were never taught.

I was raised in a Decision Laboratory. Not the kind with white lab coats and clipboards but surrounded by a community of Decision Analysis innovators at Stanford University who were inventing a structured approach to decision making that gets you more of what you want in the face of life's uncertainties. As the daughter of Decision Analysis pioneer, Prof. James Matheson, I became an unexpected byproduct of this movement; as they applied this formalized approach to business, we, the next generation, grew up naturally integrating great decision making into everyday life as thinking and feeling humans.

I was born to lead the Decision Revolution charge–to create global change, one human and one decision at a time, so we all can get more of what we want for ourselves, our families, and our communities.

With twenty years of experience in decision education, I realized we needed to better teach whole people by supporting them in integrating their unique minds and hearts in getting decision clarity and taking effective action. In 2018, my friend, Kristen Jawad, and I cofounded Clarity4Action.org to teach and coach young people, and the adults who care about them, whole-person decision-making skills.

COVID-19 arrived and wrenched us out of classrooms, alternative schools, and community centers where we had been teaching teens and equipping their parents and mentors. Faced with a pause or a pivot, I chose to refocus my energy on creating family and community Decision Laboratory leaders by teaching and coaching young adults launching their lives, parents facing new high-stakes decisions, and adults creating legacy and mentoring the young people around them.

I began my quest for a supportive community as I faced the new methods required for my success as I started over from almost ground zero; I joined a few but none like TLA. Sure, they all offered support calls, online resources, retreats, and trainings. But I had something big to share as a thought leader and through my book. In other communities, I lived in fear of the cracking whip as I sat on the coaching 'hot seat' with a leader advising me to hustle, push, and DO more with urgency. It was exhausting so I made some changes.

One day I found myself stuck in confusion and not knowing what to do next. I sat on Sara's virtual 'love seat' during a TLA call. I braced myself, my stomach clenched . . . she said, "Amy, here's my stretch for you. Take a nap."

What? Take a nap? I literally laughed out loud! The echoes from my own work teaching people to embrace themselves as whole people came back to me in Sara's comforting words.

I am so capable of doing more in my rich and fulfilling life as I balance my thought leadership, Clarity4Action.org, and my home life as a wife, mother of three kids in their twenties, caretaker for older parents, singer, and urban farmer. I can feel pulled in many directions. I took the coaching and . . . I TOOK A NAP!

As I woke, I lay in bed in the liminal space of not truly asleep or awake and there were my answers, right inside me. I had a plan! Structure, community, my pod, humor, resources, and loving and practical coaching ALL feed me. Leaning into mindset, self-compassion, and rest have 10X'd my whole life.

Since I joined TLA, I've more than doubled my email list, hosted an online interview series, launched the paid Decision Laboratory group intensive cohort, written more than half of my book, created multiple strategic alliances, and made life-long mutually supportive TLA friends. Ultimately, I see bigger possibilities for myself, my family, my work, and the world. My book launch, more stages, audience growth, and more frequent Decision Laboratory cohorts are on my horizon!

As I said earlier, YOU are the decision maker.

Stop beating yourself up for the results of your choices. Life is uncertain and can unexpectedly throw monkey wrenches into the works or provide amazing surprises that are out of your control. Your power lies in your decisions–learn how to make great ones! I was raised in a Decision Laboratory, and you can learn in one too!

At Clarity4Action.org, we have so many resources to support you! Free weekly decision coaching emails and monthly workshops with the Decision Club, The Decision Classroom self-paced online course, and The Decision Laboratory learning cohorts are available to you! Schedule a free support call infused with kindness and humor. You can also book me as a speaker for your community. Come see me at Clarity4Action.org where we have so many resources to support you-through our Decision Club, The Decision Classroom self-paced online course, and The Decision Laboratory!

Happy Decision Making!

Clarity4Action.org

Acknowledgments

Tremendous thanks to Patti Fors and the team at Muse. Thanks to the SCC team: Alex, Alexis, Amy, Audrey, (we have so many *A* names!) Hannah, Marietta, and Mary. Greatest gratitude to the incredible leaders in Thought Leader Academy-your courage inspires me daily. And at the center of my heart: Bill, Finn, and Mav.

About the Author

Sara Connell is a bestselling author and the founder of Thought Leader Academy. She has been featured on *Oprah, Good Morning America, The View,* and TEDx. Her work has appeared in *The New York Times, Forbes, Parenting,* and *Entrepreneur.* She lives in Chicago with her husband, son, Finn, and dog, Maverick.